BIZARRE TRUTHS

FACTS SO STRANGE YOU'LL SWEAR THEY'RE FICTION

Publications International, Ltd.

TABLE OF CONTENTS

CHAPTER 1

THE WEIRD WORLD OF FOOD

Would You Like Fried Worms with That?

Granted, to some people a Twinkie probably looks pretty weird. But at least Twinkies don't slither or smell like poo. Here's a sampling of some of the weirdest foods in the world.

Nutria

The nutria is a semi-aquatic rodent about the size of a cat with bright orange teeth. After World War II, they were sold in the United States as "Hoover Hogs." Since the animals chew up crops and cause erosion, in 2002 Louisiana officials offered $4 for every nutria killed. Still, their meat is rumored to be lean and tasty.

Uok

The coconut: Without it, the piña colada and macaroons wouldn't exist. Neither would the Uok, a golf ball-size, coconut-dwelling, bitter-tasting worm enjoyed by some Filipinos. Just pull one down from a tree, salt, and sauté!

Balut

If you're craving a midnight snack, skip the cheesecake and enjoy a boiled duck embryo. Folks in Cambodia will let eggs develop until the bird inside is close to hatching, and then they boil it and enjoy the egg with a cold beer.

Frog Smoothies

In Bolivia and Peru, Lake Titicaca frogs are harvested for a beverage affectionately referred to as "Peruvian Viagra." The frogs go into a blender with some spices and the resulting brown goo is served up in a tall glass. Turn on the Barry White...

Duck Blood Soup

Bright red goose blood is the main ingredient in this Vietnamese soup. A few veggies and spices round out the frothy meal.

Talk to an Expert:
Banana Gasser

Q: You gas bananas?

A: That's the short version. My work is much more precise and technical than you might think, because bananas are so perishable. Have you ever wondered how bananas can make it from other continents to your grocery store in edible shape, and yet they turn black and disgusting after three days on your kitchen counter?

Q: Now that you mention it, yes. But they are refrigerated during their cross-continental trip, right?

A: By itself, refrigeration wouldn't bring home the banana, so to speak. Banana pickers harvest them when they're green, and they're shipped in chilled containers. That's where I come in. New shipments are placed in hermetically sealed chambers, where I spray the fruit with gas to catalyze ripening. If I'm on my game, they show up at your grocery store looking like something you'd want to peel and eat either on the spot or within a couple of days.

Q: What type of gas do you use?

A: Ethylene, C2H4, which basically is what remains of the alcohol in liquor if you take out the water. Plants naturally produce ethylene, and it causes fruit to ripen. I'm in charge of manipulating the gas vents so the fruit ripens when we want it to ripen. The gas itself doesn't harm the fruit, nor does it harm people.

Q: Not to sound critical, but how hard is it to open a gas vent?

A: There's more to it than that. Here's the reality: First I have to evaluate where the bananas came from and how long they have been traveling. They go immediately into the chamber, and I have to decide how much gas to give them, what temperature to keep them at, and for how long. A given chamber's bananas need to have the same general characteristics, because one batch of fast-ripeners could cause the whole chamber of bananas to ripen too early.

Food Fight!

Sure, parties are fun, but add in massive amounts of food and a reason to throw it around, and you've got yourself an international festival! The following are some of the world's craziest food-related events.

Hunterville Huntaway Festival, Hunterville, New Zealand: The highlight of this annual October event is the Shepherd's Shemozzle, a grueling endurance and obstacle race, in which shepherds and their dogs run through a course that includes a variety of culinary challenges, such as swallowing raw eggs or downing a delicious bowl of sheep's eye mixed with cream. The winnings include a monetary prize and a supply of dog food.

La Tomatina, Buñol, Spain: On the last Wednesday in August, thousands of people descend on this sleepy little village for the world's most impressive tomato fight. Nearly 140 tons of juicy red tomatoes are trucked in from the countryside. The trucks dump off the tomatoes, the people fasten their goggles, and then the fun begins. A word of advice: Don't wear your best clothes for this one.

Ivrea Carnival and Orange Battle, Ivrea, Italy: This is just like Spain's La Tomatina, only with oranges instead of tomatoes. It occurs 40 days before Lent, and it typically involves thousands of orange-hurling celebrants. Don't forget to duck—oranges can hurt!

West Virginia RoadKill Cook-Off, Marlinton, West Virginia: This festival, which typically occurs in September, is exactly as its name suggests. One can try delicious dishes such as Thumper Meets Bumper, Asleep at the Wheel Squeal, and Tire Tread Tortillas. Bottom line: If a critter's been smacked by a vehicle, it's as good as covered with gravy. Bon appétit!

Festival Gastronomico del Gato, La Quebrada, Peru: In this small Peruvian village, every September 21 cats go from favorite pets to delicious main dishes as part of this bizarre celebration (the name translates to "Gastronomic Festival of the Cat"). Celebrants sauté Mr. Whiskers to commemorate the village's original settlers, slaves who at one time were forced to live on cat meat.

Olive Oil Wrestling Competition, Edirne, Turkey: For centuries, hundreds of burly Turks have donned trousers made of water buffalo hide, slathered themselves with slippery olive oil, and wrestled each other. These contests occur throughout the country, but the most famous tournament takes place in the town of Edirne. The winner receives a cash prize and the right to call himself "Champion of Turkey."

Night of the Radishes, Oaxaca, Mexico: This event, which takes place every December 23, is more of an art show than anything else as participants carve huge, gnarly radishes into elaborate scenes and figures. Ever wonder what the Virgin Mary would look like if carved into a radish? Here's your chance to find out.

Lopburi Monkey Festival, Lopburi, Thailand: This place is literally overrun with macaques, which in turn attract a lot of tourists. To show their appreciation, the locals host a party for the monkeys in November at the Prang Sam Yot temple. Thousands of pounds of food are presented to the pampered primates, including fruit, boiled eggs, cucumbers, and even soft drinks to wash it all down. Entrance to the festival costs 30 baht (approximately 90 cents). The ticket price includes a bamboo stick to ward off the more aggressive simians.

Demon-Chasing Ritual, Japan: Some Japanese are a bit superstitious, so every February 3, as the gloom of winter gives way to spring, they chase away the evil from the previous year through a ritual known as *setsubun*. The ceremony involves shouting "Out with the demons, in with good luck!" while tossing roasted soybeans out the front door or at a family member wearing an Oni demon mask. Participants are also supposed to eat a soybean for every year they've been alive, plus one extra for the coming year.

How Did an Umbrella Get in My Cocktail?

That pretty paper parasol may seem like nothing more than a froufrou-y finish to your mai tai or piña colada, but it once served a noble purpose. Back in the early barroom days, hanging out at the neighborhood pub was pretty much a guys-only activity. What? Bars without women? Where in the world were men able to use their cheesy pick-up lines? Believe it or not, cocktail umbrellas helped to take care of that conundrum.

In the early 1930s, bartenders at swanky island-themed watering holes like Trader Vic's and Don the Beachcomber thought up a clever little way to lure in the ladies. They concocted all sorts of fanciful cocktails and garnished them with cute paper sunshades. Sure it was a marketing ploy, but it worked. By the 1950s and 1960s, exotic decorated drinks and Polynesian-themed restaurants and clubs became part of a whole tiki culture craze. From that moment on, the ladies—and the umbrellas—were at the bar to stay.

There are plenty of guys who enjoy refreshingly fruity umbrella drinks from time to time, too. In an effort to defend their manhood, they may come up with more "technical" reasons for covering their lava flows or zombies with a colorful little canopies. Some maintain that cocktail umbrellas shade their icy, frothy, frappés from the melting effects of solar radiation. Others suggest that cocktail umbrellas prevent volatile alcohol molecules within their drinks from evaporating too quickly.

Is this a bunch of hogwash, or do cocktail umbrellas really have science on their side? Perhaps a little bit of science—but it's more likely that these umbrellas simply evoke a sunny state of mind. Every once in a while, we all need to ditch reality for that white beach, where coconuts and pineapples and maraschino cherries are ingredients in luscious libations that smell like suntan lotion—and somehow still taste really good.

The United Fruit Company

On Monday, February 3, 1975, corporate raider Eli M. Black stood before the glass window of his office on the 44th floor of the Pan American Building in New York City. As Black stood looking at the Manhattan skyline, it is possible he thought of the Honduran banana plantations that had recently been wiped out by Hurricane Fifi. Or perhaps he thought of the devalued United Fruit Company shares that were dragging down the market viability of his newly created United Brands Company. Unfortunately, nobody will ever know exactly what Eli M. Black's thoughts were the moment he sent his briefcase sailing through Pan American's glass wall and dove after it, plunging to his death on the Park Avenue pavement far below.

Before the Fall

Seven years prior, Black had purchased enough shares to become the majority stockholder of the United Fruit Company—a powerful corporation that had molded Central and South American politics for nearly one hundred years. Eli M. Black had the distinction of presiding over the final days of the United Fruit Company. The corporation, which ended so dismally, had an equally terrible beginning. In 1871, railroad speculator Henry Mieggs secured a contract with the government of Costa Rica to develop the young country's railroad system. Unfortunately, the Costa Rican government ran out of money, and the railroad remained unfinished upon Mieggs's death. His nephew, Minor C. Keith, realized that the true value of the railroad lay not in its ability to transport people, but in its ability to transport the bananas that grew plentifully along its tracks. Keith borrowed money from London banks and private investors to finish the railroad. He then acquired tax-free rights to the land adjacent to the rails and earned exclusive trading status at the country's seaports. His banana empire thus secured, Keith joined his operation with Boston Fruit's Lorenzo Dow Baker and Andrew W. Preston. This merger brought substantial financial backing as well as one of the world's largest private holdings of transport ships, known as "The Great White Fleet." With control of the railroads and shipping, the newly created United Fruit Company soon came to dominate the region's trade.

Banana Republic

In 1901, the Guatemalan government hired the United Fruit Company to handle the country's postal service. Keith realized that Guatemala, with its right-wing dictator and ample supply of cheap labor, represented the "ideal investment climate." United Fruit soon lorded over every aspect of the Guatemalan economy. It established a base of operations in its own town, Bananera, and was able to procure extremely favorable terms from a succession of pliant governments. And with that, the "banana republic" was born.

As a key tactic, United Fruit extracted rights for vast tracts of property under the premise that the region's unpredictable weather necessitated backup plantations. This resulted in large amounts of land laying fallow. Unable to farm, the majority of the populace, mostly Indian, struggled to subsist on the company's meager wages or simply had no work at all. Apologists for United Fruit cited the growth of infrastructure as well as the relatively high wages for its permanent employees, but for the average citizen, United Fruit's regional monopoly meant curtailed opportunity. Beginning in the 1920s, the company dominated life in the region so completely that locals began calling it El Pulpo—The Octopus.

The first real test of the company's power came in 1944 when the Guatemalans overthrew their oppressive dictator, Jorge Ubico, and elected reformer Dr. Juan Jose Arevalo Bermej, who was peacefully and democratically succeeded by Jacobo Arbenz. Besides building schools and improving the circumstances of the average citizen, these men (Arbenz in particular) promised to break up the vast tracks of land held by private firms and redistribute it to the populace. As it was, 90 percent of the people had access to only 10 percent of the land. United Fruit Company, the primary landlord in the region, appealed to the United States to overthrow the democratic Guatemalan government, claiming that Arbenz was allied with the Soviet Union. In 1954, a CIA-backed coup ousted Arbenz and installed a repressive right-wing dictatorial government, sparking a civil war that lasted 36 years and resulted in the deaths of hundreds of thousands of people. Many died as a result of being on a list of "dissidents" compiled by the CIA at the behest of the United Fruit Company.

In 1968, Eli M. Black bought his ill-fated shares in United Fruit. He later merged the company with his own—a move that created the United Brands Company. Financial problems, coupled with Black's mismanagement of the company, led to serious debt for the United Brands. A 1974 hurricane, which destroyed huge crops of bananas, was perhaps the final straw for Eli Black and may have been a factor in his 1975 suicide.

In 1999, three years after the Guatemalan civil war came to an end, U.S. President Bill Clinton visited the region, and during a brief stop in Guatemala City, delivered a speech in which he expressed regret for the United States' role in the country's long, debilitating struggle, stating that Washington "was wrong" to have supported Guatemalan security forces during its "dark and painful" period of instability.

By the time President Clinton made these comments, the United Fruit Company had undergone its own "dark and painful" period. The company currently carries on under Chiquita Brands International Corporation, which acquired the deceased Eli M. Black's United Brands in 1984.

The Mystery of the Fortune Cookie

The fortune cookie may be the most famous symbol of Chinese food in America. But venture over to China and you won't find an advice-filled twist of dough anywhere in sight.

A fortune cookie is to Chinese food as a stomachache is to a greasy-spoon joint: There's absolutely no question it will follow your meal. It turns out, though, that the former is far from common in the actual country of China; in fact, you might be hard-pressed to find anyone there who's even heard of one.

So where did this crunchy cookie come from? It seems there's no single proverb that holds the answer.

The Chinese Theories

Some interesting theories trace the fortune cookie's creation to the early Chinese immigrants in America as a means to carry on valued traditions from their homeland. One story even says the fortune cookie's roots originated as far back as 12th-century China, during the rule of the Yuan Dynasty.

According to that tale, rebel monks started making a special kind of moon cake, into which they'd slip secret messages to their comrades without the invading Mongols finding out. Legend has it the men baked the cakes, messages and all, then sold them to Chinese families to spread their plans for upcoming rebellions.

Another theory traces the first fortune cookie back to ancient Chinese parlor games. In these sessions, men would write proverbs on paper and then place them inside twisted pastries.

Yet another hypothesis puts the cookie credit in the hands of George Jung, founder of Los Angeles's Hong Kong Noodle Company. Jung is believed by many to have cooked up the first fortune cookies as a way to add some happiness in the dreary post-World War I era. However, some speculate the cookies may have also served as a simple distraction for Jung's guests while their food was being prepared.

The Japanese Alternative

The other school of thought claims the Japanese were actually the inventors of the fortune cookie. Researchers have found family bakeries in and around the city of

Kyoto that have been making similarly-shaped fortune crackers since the late 1800s—long before the treat first surfaced in America around 1907.

Called *tsujiura senbei* (fortune crackers) or *omikuji senbei* (written fortune crackers), the Japanese cookies do have some differences: They are larger, darker in color, and have more of a sesame-miso flavor than the vanilla-butter combo of the Chinese variety. The fortunes are also presented within the fold rather than inside the cavity. Even so, fortune-cookie devotees insist the similarities are too great to ignore.

Some Japanese families theorize that the cookies first came over to the United States around 1890, when a man named Makoto Hagiwara helped build the Japanese Tea Garden in San Francisco's Golden Gate Park. A nearby bakery called Benkyodo, Makoto's family claims, served the cookies to visitors. It was from there, they say, that other Asian restaurants in California picked up the idea, leading to its nationwide explosion.

Fortune Resistance

Wherever it began, years later the meal-closing crunchy treat still hasn't taken off within the nation of China. An American importer named Nancy Anderson began trying to change that in 1989, but she had little success. Anderson tried importing fortune cookies made in California to Hong Kong to sell to restaurants, mainly ones that cater to—surprise, surprise—foreign tourists. With added packaging requirements, translation costs, and international taxes, the cookies ended up costing more than double their worth. All factors considered, Anderson found that most restaurant owners were wary of the desserts and hesitant to make an investment; her efforts have yielded little success.

International disdain aside, though, the beloved little cookie doesn't seem to be in any danger of disappearing from Chinese custom in America—and that's one fortune you can count on.

Cold Drinks Are Unacceptable in China

Americans enjoy glasses of ice water quite frequently, especially on hot summer days. But to the Chinese, this seems strange—they much prefer their water to be piping hot.

"In the big family I was brought up in, no one would dare to pour even room temperature water," journalist Nicole Liu wrote for the *LA Times*. "Doing so would risk a chorus of criticism, with parents, aunts, cousins, and grandparents chastising you almost simultaneously: 'Cold water gives you cramps!'"

According to Liu, China's love of hot water began in 1949, when the quality of tap water wasn't very good. The government suggested boiling it to kill bacteria. "There were boiler rooms in every workplace and community, and people delivered hot water to each household," sixty-eight-year-old Li Zhenhui told Liu. "They would do it very early in the morning by filling the containers you left outside the door. They kept saying it was for our health and hygiene."

Chinese medicine has long touted the belief that hot drinks are safer and more beneficial than cold. In fact, consuming warm water is said to aid digestion, improve circulation, and relieve sore muscles. Cold water, on the other hand, is believed to cause cramps and slow down organ function. Some Chinese people find it difficult to adjust to the cooler drinks served in other parts of the world, let alone pieces of ice floating in their drinks. Hotels and airlines are starting to tweak their services. "Hotels overseas are getting hip to Chinese tourists' needs," Liu says, "adding amenities like slippers, Chinese-language newspapers, and—yes—teakettles."

Foraging Keeps Man's Digestion from Faltering

If you suffered with chronic stomach issues, how far would you go to cure yourself? A man in southeast China uses a rather startling remedy: he eats frogs and rats. Yang Dingcai claims that forty years of swallowing live tree frogs and rats has kept his digestive system running smoothly. While it seems like a rather unpleasant and extreme measure, Yang has passed his wisdom along to others who also claim it works.

One of his devotees is sixty-six-year-old Jiang Musheng, who has suffered from frequent abdominal pains and coughing since the age of twenty-six. But one day, he met Yang Dingcai, who suggested the tree frogs as a remedy, according to the *Beijing News*. "At first, Jiang Musheng did not dare to eat a live, wriggling frog, but after seeing Yang Dingcai swallow one, he ate . . . two without a thought," the paper said. "After a month of eating live frogs, his stomach pains and coughing were completely gone." According to the paper, Jiang has also added live mice and baby rats to his unusual diet.

If Beans Cause Gas, Why Can't We Use Them to Power Our Cars?

There are two ways to consider this question.

Taking the high road, we can discuss the technology that transforms biomass into ethanol, a proven fuel for cars. Beans, like corn or virtually any other organic material, contain starches and complex carbohydrates that can be refined into ethanol, a combustible alcohol blended with gasoline to become that "green" E85 fuel you've heard about. Through fermentation—and with a lot of help from science—beans and their organic cousins can also find their way into methane gas, another proven biomass automotive fuel.

But how boring is the high road?

By "causing gas," this question really refers to the process by which the consumption of beans produces that bloated feeling that escapes us as flatulence. High-fiber foods tend to cause intestinal gas, but beans seem to bear most of the blame, maybe because other world-class gas-promoters like cabbage and Brussels sprouts aren't as big a part of our diet.

The culprit in these foods is a natural family of hard-to-digest sugars called oligosaccharides. These molecules boogie their way through our small intestine largely unmolested. The merrymaking begins when they hit the large intestine. Bacteria living there strap on the feedbag, chomping away at this nutritional bounty, multiplying even. Our intestinal gas is the by-product of their digestive action.

Most of this gas is composed of odorless hydrogen, nitrogen, and carbon dioxide. In some humans—about 30 percent of the adult population—this process also produces methane.

Ethanol isn't a part of the oligosaccharide equation. But hydrogen and methane are, and they're flammable gases. In fact, hydrogen is another player in the fuel-of-the-future derby and already powers experimental fuel-cell vehicles.

So order that chili and fill 'er up. Beans in your Beemer! Legumes for your Lexus! Not so fast, burrito boy. Setting aside the daunting biotechnical hurdle of actually capturing bean-bred flatulence from a person's, um, backside, the challenge becomes one of volume and storage.

Human flatulence simply doesn't contain hydrogen or methane in quantities sufficient to fuel anything more than a blue flame at a frat party. Even if we did generate enough of these gases to power a car, they'd have to be collected and carted around in high-pressure tanks to be effective as fuels.

Human biochemistry is a wonderful thing, but it isn't yet a backbone of the renewable-energy industry. For that, breathe a sigh of relief.

Twelve Months of Food

JANUARY

* Gourmet Coffee Month
* Oatmeal Month
* Soup Month
* Wheat Bread Month
* Chocolate-Covered Cherry Day (January 3)
* English Toffee Day (January 8)
* Peanut Brittle Day (January 26)

FEBRUARY

* Cherry Month
* Fabulous Florida Strawberry Month
* Grapefruit Month
* Sweet Potato Month
* Bubble Gum Day (February 1)
* Solo Diners Eat Out Week (February 1–7)
* Gumdrop Day (February 15)
* Chili Day (February 22)

MARCH

* Celery Month
* Frozen Food Month
* Noodle Month
* Peanut Month
* Sauce Month
* American Chocolate Week (third week in March)

APRIL

* Fresh Florida Tomato Month
* Grilled Cheese Sandwich Month
* Pecan Month
* Soft Pretzel Month
* Soy Foods Month
* Licorice Day (April 12)
* Jelly Bean Day (April 22)
* Egg Salad Week (the week after Easter)

MAY

* Asparagus Month
* Barbecue Month
* Chocolate Custard Month
* Egg Month
* Hamburger Month
* Salad Month
* Salsa Month
* Strawberry Month
* Sweet Vidalia Month
* Raisin Week (May 1–7)
* Eat Dessert First Week (May 1–7)
* Eat What You Want Day (May 11)
* Apple Pie Day (May 13)
* Chocolate Chip Day (May 15)
* Taffy Day (May 23)

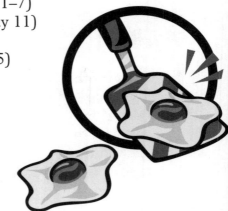

JUNE

* Candy Month
* Dairy Month
* Iced Tea Month
* Papaya Month
* Soul Food Month
* Steak House Month
* Turkey Lovers' Month
* Vinegar Day (June 16)
* Cheese Week (last week in June)

JULY

* Baked Beans Month
* Blueberry Month
* Horseradish Month
* Hot Dog Month
* Peach Month
* Gummi Worm Day (July 15)
* Lollipop Day (July 20)
* Ice Cream Day—aka Sundae Sunday
  (third Sunday in July)
* Drive-Thru Day (July 24)

AUGUST

* Get Acquainted with Kiwi Fruit Month
* Catfish Month
* Sandwich Month
* Watermelon Day (August 3)
* Mustard Day (August 4)
* S'mores Day (August 10)

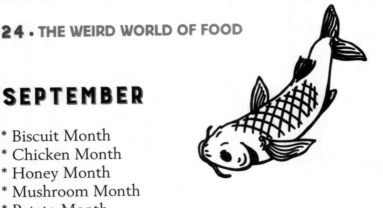

SEPTEMBER

* Biscuit Month
* Chicken Month
* Honey Month
* Mushroom Month
* Potato Month
* Rice Month
* Waffle Week (September 2–8)
* International Eat an Apple Day (September 15)

OCTOBER

* Celebrate Sun-Dried Tomatoes Month
* Eat Country Ham Month
* Apple Month
* Caramel Month
* Chili Month
* Cookie Month
* Dessert Month
* Pasta Month
* Pickled Peppers Month
* Pizza Month
* Popcorn Poppin' Month
* Pork Month
* Pretzel Month
* Seafood Month
* Chestnut Week (second week in October)
* World Egg Day (second Friday in October)
* Candy Corn Day (October 30)

NOVEMBER

* Fun with Fondue Month
* Georgia Pecan Month
* Peanut Butter Lovers' Month
* Pepper Month
* Pomegranate Month
* Raisin Bread Month
* Fig Week (November 1–7)
* Bundt Day (November 15)
* Homemade Bread Day (November 17)

DECEMBER

* Cookie Cutter Week (December 1–7)
* Gluten-Free Baking Week (week before Christmas)
* Chocolate-Covered Anything Day (December 16)
* Candy Cane Day (December 26)

The International Connoisseur of McDonald's

For most of us, McDonald's is a place we stop at when we're in a hurry and don't have time for anything else. But for Canadian software engineer James McGowan, the fast-food chain is an obsession. He has traveled to fifty-three different countries just to sample the regional dishes found in each country's McDonald's restaurants. He writes about his travels on his blog, *Traveling McD's*.

McGowan has sampled foods like a creme brulee Mc-Flurry in Singapore, salmon burger and teriyaki rice in Thailand, tofu nuggets in Japan, churros in South Korea, and poutine in Montreal.

McGowan reviews all of the foods he tries, and not all of it is to his liking. The lychee pie in Kuala Lumpur, for instance, got a zero-star rating. "The flavor was far more acidic than a pie filling should be, and just didn't go well with the fried crust at all," he wrote. He also wasn't a fan of the "disgusting" tuna pie in Thailand, "chewy" home-style chips in Copenhagen, or the thick and syrupy Mc-Fizz in Singapore. But McGowan has plenty of favorites, too, like the matcha McFlurry in Singapore and a cheese panini in Tahiti.

McGowan hopes to soon visit McDonald's restaurants in Oman, Mongolia, Qatar, and Vietnam. "Strangers say, if you're fortunate enough to go to all these countries, why do you waste it on McDonald's?" he told the *Wall Street Journal*. "I like sharing online. People seem to enjoy it." Plus, he adds, "I don't drink. I don't smoke. This is my vice."

I Scream, You Scream, We All Scream for Ice Cream (Cones)

The story of the first ice-cream cone has become part of American mythology. The stock story is that a young vendor at the 1904 St. Louis World's Fair ran out of dishes. Next to him was waffle-maker Ernest Hamwi. Hamwi got the idea to roll his waffles into a cone, and now, more than a century later, we're reaping his legacy.

But the ice-cream cone wasn't just born of convenience or a vendor's poor planning. Germs played a role, too. Italian immigrants spearheaded the introduction of ice cream to the general public, first in Europe and then in the United States. Called *hokey pokey men* (from an Italian phrase), these street vendors sold "penny licks," a small glass of ice cream that cost a single penny. The vendors wiped the glass with a rag after the customer was done and then served the next person. Unsurprisingly, people got sick.

Today, cones come in many varieties, but in 1904, Hamwi was making *zalabia*, a cross between a waffle and a wafer covered in sugar or syrup. He called his creation a *cornucopia* (a horn-of-plenty, a symbol of autumn harvest), and after the fair, he founded the Cornucopia Waffle Company with a business partner. A few years later, he started his own company, the Missouri Cone Co., and finally named his rolled-up waffles "ice-cream cones." How sweet it is!

CHAPTER 2

SPORTING ANOMALIES

PETA Wouldn't Approve of This Sport

Imagine a game in which the "ball" is the carcass of a goat—decapitated, dehoofed, and soaked overnight in cold water to make it stiff. Such a game really exists, and it's called buzkashi.

Buzkashi is the national sport of Afghanistan. In addition to the interesting choice of a ball, the players in this rough-and-tumble game are mounted on horseback and wear traditional Uzbek garb: turbans, robes, and scarves around their waists. There's no complicated playbook, only a minimally regimented strategy that requires—no, encourages—no-holds-barred violence. The referees carry rifles, in case things really get out of hand. The field has no set boundaries; spectators are in constant danger of being trampled. The objective is to gain possession of the goat and carry it to a designated goal. And the winning players cook and eat the carcass.

Buzkashi translates to "goat pulling" and likely evolved from ordinary herding. It originated with nomadic Turkic peoples who moved west from China and Mongolia from the 10th to 15th centuries. Today, it's played mainly in Afghanistan, but you can also find folks yanking the ol' carcass in northwestern China and in the Muslim republics north of Afghanistan.

The game has two basic forms: modern and traditional. The modern involves teams of ten to 12 riders. In the traditional form, it's every man for himself. Both require a combination of strength and expert horsemanship.

The competitions often are sponsored by khans ("traditional elites") who gain or lose status based on the success of the events. And in this case, success is defined by how little or how much mayhem erupts. Biting, hairpulling, grabbing another rider's reins, and using weapons are prohibited in buzkashi. Anything else goes.

A Royal Flush

Every year at the end of January, rumors begin to swirl that the sewer systems in several major cities fail due to the number of toilets that are flushed during halftime of the Super Bowl.

A Mad Dash

During Super Bowl XVIII in 1984, a water main in Salt Lake City ruptured, dampening the sporting spirit in that community. The next day, conversations around office water coolers were rife with rumors that toilet trauma, prompted by a flood of beverage-logged football fans all using the facilities at the same time, had caused the sewer systems of numerous cities to clog up. Such a myth would almost make sense if it were applied to the final of the World Cup of Soccer, where there is continuous action without stoppages of any kind until the halftime break. But anyone who has sat through the six-plus-hour spectacle known as the Super Bowl realizes that there is no merit to this tall tale. The North American brand of football—especially the game played on that particular Sunday—has numerous breaks, pauses, and lapses throughout. So to suggest there is a simultaneous dash to the latrine at any time during this all-day marathon is silly.

The Tennis Star Who Wasn't

No one can accuse *Sports Illustrated* of not having a sense of humor. For laughs, it invented an attractive, camera-ready tennis star to rival Anna Kournikova. Her name was Simonya Popova.

Sports Satire

A September 2002 issue of *Sports Illustrated* told of an unstoppable 17-year-old tennis force named Simonya Popova, a Russian from Uzbekistan and a media dream: 6'1", brilliant at the game, fluent in English, candid, busty, and blonde. She came from an appealing late-Soviet proletarian background and had a father who was often quoted in Russian-nuanced English. But she wouldn't be competing in the U.S. Open—her father forbade it until she turned 18.

The magazine verged on rhapsody as it compared Popova to Ashley Harkleroad, Daniela Hantuchová, Elena

Dementieva, and Jelena Dokic. Editors claimed that, unlike Popova, all of these women were public-relations disappointments to both the Women's Tennis Association (WTA) and sports marketing because they chose to resist media intrusions to concentrate on playing good tennis. As a result, U.S. tennis boiled down to Venus and Serena Williams, trailed by a pack of hopefuls and won't-quite-get-theres. The gushing article concluded with this line: "If only she existed."

Just Kidding!

Popova *was* too good to be true. The biography was fiction, and her confident gaze simply showcased someone's digital artistry.

Some people got it. Many didn't, including the media. They bombarded the WTA with calls: Who was Popova and why wasn't she in the Open? The article emphasized what many thought—the WTA was desperate for the next young tennis beauty. WTA spokesperson Chris DeMaria called the story "misleading and irritating" and "disrespectful to the great players we have." Complaining that some people didn't read to the end of articles, he said, "We're a hot sport right now and we've never had to rely on good looks."

Sports Illustrated claimed it was all in grand fun. It hardly needed to add that it was indulging in puckish social commentary on the sexualization of women's tennis.

The Worst Team in Baseball History

Who was the worst team in major league baseball history? The 1962 New York Mets and their record of 40-120? Ha! The 42-112 Pittsburgh Pirates of 1952? Please. The 2003 Detroit Tigers, who went 43-119? C'mon.

No, the worst team in professional baseball history was the 1899 Cleveland Spiders, whose record of 20-134 gave them a scintillating .130 winning percentage. They were good (or bad) enough to finish a mere 84 games out of first place. Yet just four years prior the Spiders had been the best team in baseball. What happened?

Along Came Some Spiders

The Cleveland Spiders, so called because of the skinny appearance of many of their players, began life in baseball's National League in 1889. In 1892, led by future pitching great Denton True "Cy" Young (who was bought by the team for $300 and a new suit), the Spiders finished second in the league. In 1895, the Spiders won the Temple Cup, the forerunner to the World Series.

However, despite the large crowds that would attend Sunday games, playing baseball on that day was still controversial. In 1897, the entire Spiders team was thrown into the pokey for playing baseball on the Sabbath. The following season, Cleveland was forced to shift most of their Sunday games to other cities. Attendance suffered, and the team stumbled to a record of 81-68.

Web Spinning

One other factor contributed to the Spiders' demise: Syndicate baseball. This meant that it was acceptable for owners of one National League team to own stock in another. Inevitably, the team with the better attendance and players drew most of the owner's attention and finances, while the lesser team suffered.

Syndicate baseball arrived in Cleveland in early 1899, when owner Frank Robison bought the St. Louis Browns at a sheriff's auction. He decided that St. Louis was a better market than Cleveland, and so he shipped all of the best Spiders there and renamed the new group—in case anyone missed the point—the Perfectos. Meanwhile, the absent Spiders were replaced by, well, anybody.

Robison's brother Stanley was put in charge of the team. Stanley started off on the wrong foot with Cleveland fans by stating that he intended to operate the Spiders "as a sideshow." Faced with that encouraging news, less than 500 fans turned out for Cleveland's Opening Day double-header. Not surprisingly, the Spiders lost both games. The rout had begun.

And what a rout it was! After the first 38 games, the Spiders had 30 losses. Deciding that third baseman/manager Lave Cross was the problem, Robison sent him to St. Louis (which actually was a reward). With virtually no one showing up for the games, Stanley locked the Cleveland ballpark and announced that the Spiders would play their remaining "home" games on the road.

Woebegone Wanderers

The dismal team—now dubbed the "Wanderers," "Exiles," and "Foresakens"—won just 12 more games the entire season. At one point they lost 24 games straight, which is still a record. They were so bad that after the Spiders beat the Baltimore Orioles, the Orioles' pitcher was fined and suspended. In the midst of all this, Cleveland sportswriter Elmer Bates compiled a tongue-in-cheek list of reasons to follow the Spiders. Among them:

1. There is everything to hope for and nothing to fear.

2. Defeats do not disturb one's sleep.

3. There is no danger of any club passing you.

4. You are not [always] asked . . . "What was the score?" People take it for granted that you lost.

On the last day of their season, a 19-year-old cigar stand clerk was the pitcher for the Spiders; the team lost 19-3. After the game, the Spiders presented the team travel secretary with a diamond locket because, as the dedication said, he "had the misfortune to watch us in all our games." The following year Cleveland was dropped from the National League.

Nine Odd Sporting Events from Around the World

Cheese Rolling

If you're a whiz at cheese rolling, you may want to head to Brockworth in Gloucestershire, England, at the annual

Cooper's Hill Cheese Roll held each May. The ancient festival dates back hundreds of years and involves pushing and shoving a large, mellow, seven- to eight-pound wheel of ripe Gloucestershire cheese downhill in a race to the bottom. With the wheels of cheese reaching up to 70 miles per hour, runners chase, tumble, and slide down the hill after their cheese but don't usually catch up until the end. The winner gets to take home his or her cheese, while the runners-up get cash prizes.

Toe Wrestling

This little piggy went to the World Toe Wrestling Championship held annually in July in Derbyshire, England. Contestants sit facing each other at a "toedium"—a stadium for toes—and try to push each other's bare foot off a small stand called a "toesrack." Three-time champion Paul Beech calls himself the "Toeminator." Toe wrestling began in the town of Wetton in 1970, and the international sport is governed by the World Toe Wrestling Organization, which once applied for Olympic status but was rejected.

Tuna Throwing

Popular in Australia, tuna throwing requires contestants to whirl a frozen tuna around their heads with a rope and then fling it like an Olympic hammer thrower. Since 1998, the record holder has been former Olympic hammer thrower Sean Carlin, with a tuna toss of 122 feet. With $7,000 in prize money overall, the event is part of Tunarama, an annual festival held in late January in Port Lincoln, South Australia. Animal rights activists will be pleased to know that the tuna are spoiled fish that stores refused to sell.

Pooh Sticks

Christopher Robin knows that pooh sticks is not a hygiene problem but rather a game played with Winnie the Pooh. The game consists of finding a stick, dropping it into a river, and then seeing how long it takes to get to the finish line. There is even an annual World Pooh Sticks Championship held in mid-March in Oxfordshire, England. Individual event winners receive gold, silver, and bronze medals, and a team event has attracted competitors from Japan, Latvia, and the Czech Republic.

Man Versus Horse Marathon

The Man Versus Horse Marathon is an annual race between humans and horse-and-rider teams held in early June in the Welsh town of Llanwrtyd Wells. The event started in 1980 when a pub keeper overheard two men debating which was faster in a long race—man or horse. Slightly shorter than a traditional marathon, the 22-mile course is filled with many natural obstacles, and horses win nearly every year. But in 2004, Huw Lobb made history as the first runner to win the race (in 2 hours, 5 minutes, and 19 seconds), taking the £25,000 (about $47,500) prize, which was the accumulation of 25 yearly £1,000 prizes that had not been claimed. Apparently, the horse doesn't get to keep its winnings.

Bull Running

While bullfighting is popular in many countries, the sport of bull running (which should really be called bull outrunning) is pretty much owned by Pamplona, Spain. The event dates back to the 13th and 14th centuries as a combination of festivals honoring St. Fermin and bullfighting. Every morning for a week in July, the half-mile race is on between six bulls and hundreds of people. Most of the participants try to get as close to the bulls as possible, and many think it's good luck to touch one.

Tomato Tossing

Tomatoes aren't just for salads and sauce anymore. La Tomatina is a festival held in late August in the small town of Buñol, Spain, where approximately 30,000 people come from all over the world to pelt one another with nearly 140 tons of overripe tomatoes. The fruit fight dates back to the mid-1940s but was banned under Francisco Franco, then returned in the 1970s after his death. After two hours of tomato-tossing at La Tomatina, there are no winners or losers, only stains and sauce, and the cleanup begins.

Human Tower Building

If you enjoy watching cheerleaders form human pyramids, you'll love the castellers, people who compete to form giant human towers at festivals around Catalonia, Spain. Castellers form a solid foundation of packed bodies, linking arms and hands together in an intricate way that holds several tons and softens the fall in case the tower collapses, which is not uncommon. Up to eight more levels of people are built, each layer standing on the shoulders of the people below. The top levels are made up of children and when complete, the castell resembles a human Leaning Tower of Pisa.

Wife Carrying Championship

During the Wife Carrying Championship, held annually in Sonkajärvi, Finland, contestants carry a woman—it needn't be their wife—over an 832-foot course with various obstacles en route. Dropping the woman incurs a 15-second penalty, and the first team to reach the finish line receives the grand prize—the weight of the "wife" in beer! This bizarre event traces its origins to the 19th century when a local gang of bandits commonly stole women from neighboring villages.

Extreme Sports: Playing on the Edge

The following activities exist well off sport's mainstream path. From 1,000 feet below ground to at least that high overhead, endorphin-hounds risk it all in pursuit of "epic" moments.

"Swabbing" the Swabbie

Water (or sea) jousting captures all the action of medieval jousting without that sport's messy mauling and death. Nevertheless, it features fearsome competitors such as the "Unrootable" Casimir Castaldo and Vincent Cianni, "the man of 100 victories." The drill is simple: Two boats are rowed toward each other. When helm nears helm, competitors perched on protruding platforms draw their lances and get busy. Last one standing gets the girl, or at least a moment of glory. And the vanquished? That wet critter gets to joust another day.

The sport dates back to 2780 BC, when Egyptian bas-reliefs depicted nautical jousts that were possibly a genuine form of warfare. The most prestigious event is the Tournament de la Saint-Louis held in Sète, France, every August. Since 1743 it has attracted hordes of enthusiastic followers who come to see their least favorite competitors get "bumped off."

I Can't Believe I Ate the Whole Thing

Nathan's Famous is the name most associated with eating contests, but there are many more out there. At the 2007 Coney Island event, 230-pound Californian Joey "Jaws" Chestnut rammed 66 hot dogs and buns down his gullet in 12 minutes to set a new world record.

Consider these impossible-sounding world marks: 22 slices of 16-inch-diameter pizza downed in ten minutes by 190-pound Chicagoan Patrick Bertoletti in August 2007. Or how about 8.31 pounds of Armour Vienna sausage wolfed down in ten minutes? This eat feat was accomplished by petite Sonya Thomas in May 2005. At 105 pounds, Thomas proves far and away that physical size is not necessary to produce records.

Underwater Pursuits

Scuba diving is risky business, but cave diving ups the ante even more. Here practitioners do underwater what spelunkers do underground. The difference? If a spelunker gets lost, it's usually an inconvenience. To a cave diver equipped with limited oxygen, it can mean death.

Experts explore ever deeper and more distant passages, but even the greatest can have an off day. Sheck Exley of Jacksonville, Florida, was a pioneer in cave diving. The 45-year-old had captured numerous world records in the sport before he met with tragedy in 1994 at Zacatón, a forbiddingly deep sinkhole in Mexico. When his body was recovered a few days later, his depth gauge showed a maximum depth of 879 feet. To many, he was the absolute best; unfortunately, statistics show he probably won't be the last.

Peak Performance

Ordinary skiing features lifts that take people to the top of groomed trails, but heliskiing uses helicopters to deliver skiers to wild, often untouched terrain. Reaching a mountain's absolute peak opens up a brave new world of virgin powder and incomparable alpine views, as well as extreme avalanches and bone breaks. The latter two occur often enough that outfitters generally provide clients with GPS transponders to help locate them in the event of an accident or avalanche.

Heliskiing isn't cheap. On average, heliskiers can expect to pay between $500 and $1,000 for three to four full runs. But it's worth it, according to aficionados who are willing to pay the price and risk their lives for solitude on the slopes and the chance to ski thousands more feet per run.

The Ultimate (Ground) Rush

B.A.S.E. jumping—an acronym for Building, Antenna, Span, Earth—is the practice of skydiving from these four different, ground-anchored points. Popularized by endorphin-junkies in the 1970s, the sport continues to grow despite inherent risks.

Though no single venue is typical, West Virginia's famed New River Gorge Bridge is revered as a glorious step-off spot. Once there, jumpers toss themselves into the 876-foot high abyss. Free-fall time before chutes open? About four seconds. Time from takeoff to "splat!" if they don't? Approximately eight seconds. Since 1981, more than 116 unlucky B.A.S.E. jumpers have been killed pursuing the sport.

Shredding the Tarmac

Street luge (aka butt-boarding) is where speed freaks go when the melt is on. As with winter luge, the first to reach the bottom wins. Unlike the snowy version, steep paved roadways of varying lengths are used for propulsion.

Street lugers lay flat on their backs, but because there is no ice, they ride an elongated version of a skateboard. Steering is accomplished with leg pressure and by shifting body weight.

Born in the 1970s by skateboarders searching for greater speed, a modern "boarder" can hit speeds in excess of 70 miles per hour, with handling that boggles the mind. Even so, accidents happen, and when they do, they're generally spectacular.

Freestyle Walking

Despite its unimposing name, freestyle walking represents an all-new level of extreme sport. Using an urban landscape as their playground, practitioners outfitted with nothing more than their bodies fluidly jump from building to building, swing from fences, dive over benches and walls, and hop, skip, and jump over just about everything else. Unaware observers might think they're watching the filming of an action flick.

The extreme part of this sport kicks in when grip is lost, distances are misjudged, or Murphy's Law comes into play. Since the early 1990s, the sport has attracted a youth culture that constantly raises the bar by attempting ever-more dicey moves.

Wakeboarding Gets Gnarly

Occasionally, an expert in a given sport asks, "How can I make this less safe?" This seems to be the case with rail-sliding, a relatively new addition to the wakeboardist's bag of tricks.

Here's how it works: A wakeboarder is towed by a boat, as if waterskiing, toward a stationary rail in the water. The widths of these beams vary from a few inches to more than a foot, and some reach 90 feet in length. At the last second, the boarder bunny hops on top of this slicker-than-glass surface, landing his board in a standing position with feet straddling the rail.

If all goes well, he slides along to glory. If not, a host of really bad things can happen, including back-crushing "kickouts" (backward falls onto the rail), agonizing face plants (a kickout performed in reverse), and worse.

A Pick and a Prayer

Leave it to rock climbers to devise ever-more dangerous pastimes. Ice climbing raises the bar and offers a way to climb in the dreaded winter off-season.

With pickax in hand and crampons strapped to feet, the climber advances . . . until he or she hears an ominous cracking sound. Though this scenario is infrequent, it does happen. When it doesn't, ice climbers enjoy the same rush as rock climbers.

With soft ice, falling ice, and avalanches posing additional risks, ice climbing is thought to be even more perilous than rock climbing. But that doesn't stop the adventurous from taking a swing at it—the swing of an ax, that is.

Down the Chute

Imagine whooshing down an icy luge track at breakneck speed, the course moving by in a blur. Now imagine lying headfirst on a sled and doing the same. Welcome to skeleton luge, where one false move produces one serious headache.

Competitors, or "sliders," must first run 100 feet while pushing their sleds. Then they jump aboard, navigate the course with their body movements, and hope all goes according to plan. The sled follows a steeply banked track, and there are no brakes. Fastest time wins the day. After hitting speeds of 80 miles per hour and pulling up to four Gs on a skeleton luge, the neighborhood toboggan hill will never look the same.

Getting into It

Straight from New Zealand comes zorbing, an offbeat ball sport invented in the 1990s that's practiced inside a giant ball. Here's the drill: The zorbian (zorbing enthusiast) straps himself inside a fully inflated plastic ball. Then, with common sense jettisoned in favor of high adventure, an assistant sets the ball rolling down a steep hill. Happy shrieks can be heard as the zorbian attains speeds up to 25 miles per hour. If the ball veers off course or takes a bad bounce, shrieks of a far different sort can be heard. Clearly on a roll, this sport has spread into Norway, Sweden, Switzerland, China, Japan, England, and the United States, among other countries.

CHAPTER 3

SILLY BUT TRUE

A Jelly of a President!

It's well known that President John F. Kennedy had an affinity for sweet things (ahem). What isn't known is that he referred to himself as a jelly doughnut in a landmark speech.

When JFK journeyed to Berlin in 1963, he had already survived the debacle of the Bay of Pigs and withstood the anxiety of the Cuban Missile Crisis—all while maneuvering through the frigid waters of the Cold War. His trip to West Germany was seen as an endorsement of both democracy and détente, and the speech he was scheduled to deliver to the German people was expected to be one of the most influential of his presidency. When he concluded his commentary with the words "I am a Berliner" in the native language of his listeners, it was regarded as a key moment in his thousand days in office.

Kennedy's speech was a plea for the freedom of all people, and he used Berlin as a symbol of that freedom. To emphasize the point, he used the phrase "Ich bin ein Berliner" in an attempt to convey his unity with the people of Berlin. What he didn't realize is that the word *Berliner* could also be used as the word for *jelly doughnut*. By using the phrase the way he did, Kennedy could be accused of indicating that he was a jam-filled pastry rather than a participant in the city's struggle for freedom.

The words were scripted for Kennedy by a respected interpreter, Robert H. Lochner, who was carefully tutored on the proper phrasing. Lochner was informed that while a citizen of Berlin would say, "Ich bin Berliner," that would not be the correct terminology for a non-citizen like Kennedy to use. This is why the preposition "ein" was added to the text, even though it could be loosely construed as a denotation of a doughy delicacy.

Non-Required Reading

Read any good books lately? If you've already read everything by Edgar Allan Poe, Agatha Christie, J. K. Rowling, and Dean Koontz, here's a list of some of the more offbeat titles you may have missed as well as the year they were published:

How To Cook Husbands, Elizabeth Strong Worthington, 1899

Do Snakes Have Legs?, Bert Cunningham, 1934

Teach Yourself Alcoholism, Meier Glatt, 1975

Sex Life of the Foot and Shoe, William Rossi, 1977

How to Make Love While Conscious, Guy Kettelhack, 1993

Lightweight Sandwich Construction, J. M. Davies, 2001

Bombproof Your Horse, Sgt. Rick Pelicano, 2004

In Random Fashion

* 37 percent of Americans believe the U.S. government is in contact with aliens.

* There are places in Panama where the sun rises over the Pacific and sets in the Atlantic.

* If left unchecked, 100 fleas can produce 500,000 offspring.

* Vampire bats can—and do—drink their sleeping victims' blood for 30 minutes without waking them.

* Since 1884, there have been 23 documented cases of humans born with true vestigial tails.

* The U.S. Mint has made enough pennies to circle Earth more than 137 times.

* The United States ranks seventh in the world in deaths by power lawn mower.

* Seven percent of American workers admit to wasting more than three hours each workday.

* Like fingerprints, all tongue prints are unique.

* You can form the number 12,345,678,987,654,321 by multiplying 111,111,111 by 111,111,111.

* Tree crickets sing in exact mathematic ratio to the temperature of the air. No need for a thermometer on a summer night—just count the number of chirps a cricket makes in 15 seconds, add 40, and the result will be the current temperature in degrees Fahrenheit.

How to Hypnotize a Chicken

Gently hold a chicken on its side on a flat surface, lightly securing its head. Move either your index finger or a small stick back and forth in front of the bird, about four or five inches from its beak. Keep the motion parallel to its head. Soon, the bird will fall into a "trance," which is easily lifted when you release the chicken.

20 Silly and Unusual U.S. Laws

1. In Fairbanks, Alaska, it is illegal to serve alcohol to a moose.

2. In Glendale, Arizona, it is illegal to drive a car in reverse, so virtually everyone in a mall parking lot is breaking the law.

3. In San Francisco, California, it is illegal to wipe your car with used underwear. So, is it okay to use clean underwear?

4. In Quitman, Georgia, it's illegal to change the clothes on a storefront mannequin unless the shades are down.

5. In South Bend, Indiana, it's illegal for monkeys to smoke cigarettes. Apparently cigars are okay, but only if the monkey goes outside.

6. In New Orleans, Louisiana, it's against the law to gargle in public.

7. In Boston, Massachusetts, it's illegal to take a bath unless one has been ordered by a physician to do so.

8. In Minnesota, women may face 30 days in jail for impersonating Santa Claus.

9. In Hornytown, North Carolina, it's illegal to open a massage parlor.

10. In Fargo, North Dakota, it's illegal to lie down and fall asleep with your shoes on.

11. In Oxford, Ohio, it is illegal for a woman to disrobe in front of a man's picture. Is it legal if his eyes are closed in the photo?

12. In Oklahoma, people who make ugly faces at dogs can be fined or jailed. Apparently, it's okay for bulldogs to make ugly faces at people because they can't help it.

13. In Marion, Oregon, ministers are forbidden from eating garlic or onions before delivering a sermon.

14. In Morrisville, Pennsylvania, women need a permit to wear makeup.

15. In South Dakota, it's illegal to lie down and fall asleep in a cheese factory.

16. At restaurants in Memphis, Tennessee, all pie must be eaten on the premises, as it is illegal to take unfinished pie home.

17. In Utah, birds have the right-of-way on all highways.

18. In Seattle, Washington, women who sit on men's laps on buses or trains without placing a pillow between them face an automatic six-month jail term.

19. In Nicholas County, West Virginia, no clergy member may tell jokes or humorous stories from the pulpit during church services.

20. In St. Croix, Wisconsin, women are not allowed to wear anything red in public.

Crime-Busting Beatles

As more than 74 million people watched the Beatles' first performance on the *Ed Sullivan* Show in February 1964, it's said that felons in the United States refrained from thugging long enough to case the Fab Four.

Missing the Joke

Alas, the Beatles' career as crime-countering crusaders is highly overrated. B. F. Henry, a writer for the *Washington Post*, perpetrated this myth with his poison pen. Henry wrote a sneering and satirical editorial about the Beatles' TV debut, concluding that this was the only good thing about their appearance: "During the hour they were on *Ed Sullivan*, there wasn't a single hubcap stolen in America." As with most scripted sarcasm, the message went soaring over the heads of Henry's readers, who took the comment at face value. The quote gained national prominence when *Newsweek* reprinted it—without the nuanced derision.

Soon, myth mongers were inferring that between eight and nine o'clock on that Sunday evening, crime and time stood still. Even George Harrison believed the hype, stating, "While we were on, there were no reported crimes, or at least very few. When the Beatles were on *Ed Sullivan*, even the criminals had a rest for ten minutes."

Hubcap Hullabaloo

The simple truth is that crime and criminal patterns are not measured by the hour, so there is no way to accurately gauge whether the streets in the United States were safer while the Beatles tossed tunes at their adoring fans. As for the hubcap issue, a guy named Lawrence Fellenz, of Alexandria, Virginia, reported that all four of his were stolen off his vehicle that very same night. Hmm . . . that's one for each Beatle, so the question becomes: Were John, Paul, George, and Ringo really the ones performing on Sullivan's stage that evening? That's another rumor for another time.

27 Silly Presidential Nicknames

PRESIDENT	NICKNAME
1. James Monroe	Last Cocked Hat
2. John Quincy Adams	Old Man Eloquent
3. Martin Van Buren	The Little Magician; Martin Van Ruin
4. John Tyler	His Accidency
5. Zachary Taylor	Old Rough and Ready
6. Millard Fillmore	His Accidency
7. James Buchanan	The Bachelor President; Old Buck

8. Andrew Johnson — King Andy; Sir Veto

9. Ulysses S. Grant — Useless; Unconditional Surrender

10. Rutherford B. Hayes — Rutherfraud Hayes; His Fraudulency

11. James Garfield — The Preacher; The Teacher President

12. Grover Cleveland — Uncle Jumbo; His Obstinacy

13. Benjamin Harrison — Little Ben; White House Iceberg

14. William McKinley — Wobbly Willie; Idol of Ohio

15. Woodrow Wilson — The Schoolmaster

16. Warren Harding — Wobbly Warren

17. Herbert Hoover — The Great Engineer

18. Harry Truman — The Haberdasher

19. John F. Kennedy — King of Camelot

20. Lyndon B. Johnson — Big Daddy

21. Richard M. Nixon — Tricky Dick

22. Gerald Ford — The Accidental President

23. Jimmy Carter — The Peanut Farmer

24. Ronald Reagan — Dutch; The Gipper; The Great Communicator

25. George H. W. Bush — Poppy

26. Bill Clinton — Bubba; Slick Willie; The Comeback Kid

27. George W. Bush — Junior; W; Dubya

23 Silly City Names

1. Bird-in-Hand, Pennsylvania
2. What Cheer, Iowa
3. Ding Dong, Texas
4. Elbow, Saskatchewan
5. Monkeys Eyebrow, Kentucky
6. Flin Flon, Manitoba
7. Goofy Ridge, Illinois
8. Hell, Michigan
9. Intercourse, Pennsylvania
10. Joe Batt's Arm, Newfoundland
11. Cut and Shoot, Texas
12. Jackass Flats, Nevada
13. Owl's Head, Maine
14. Peculiar, Missouri
15. Placentia, Newfoundland
16. Saint-Louis-du-Ha! Ha!, Quebec
17. Suck-Egg Hollow, Tennessee
18. Swastika, Ontario
19. Tightwad, Missouri
20. Toad Suck, Arkansas
21. Truth or Consequences, New Mexico
22. Wahoo, Nebraska
23. Paint Lick, Kentucky

Bugsy Siegel's "Screen Test"

When mobster Bugsy Siegel acted out a scene at the behest of actor pal George Raft, the results proved eye-opening. Much to the surprise of all, the gangster could really act. Unfortunately, Siegel never pursued acting, choosing instead to remain on his murderous course. This begs the rather obvious question: "What if?"

In the annals of the underworld, there was perhaps no one more dapper, or more ruthless, than Benjamin "Bugsy" Siegel (1906–1947). Nearly six feet tall, with piercing blue eyes that melted the heart of many a woman, Siegel had movie-star looks and savoir faire that disguised a temperament that could easily be described as hair-triggered. During his hard-lived life, Siegel committed nearly every crime in the book and was implicated by the FBI for more than 30 murders.

Born Benjamin Hymen Siegelbaum, the up-and-coming mobster picked up the nickname "Bugsy" (the slang term bugs means "crazy") for his high level of viciousness. Siegel hated the tag, considering it a low-class connection to his hardscrabble youth, and threatened to kill anyone who used it in his presence. Still, the mobster was said to be a natural born charmer who never seemed at a loss for companionship, female or otherwise.

One of Siegel's closest friends was Hollywood actor George Raft, who was known for such memorable films as *Scarface* (1932), *I Stole a Million* (1939), and *They Drive by Night* (1940). The two had both grown up on the gritty streets of New York City's Lower East Side. Throughout their lives, the pair would engage in a form of mutual admiration. For example, Raft's movie career featured many mob-related roles. So, when he needed the proper tough-guy "inspiration," the actor would mimic mannerisms and inflections that he picked up from his real-life mobster pals. Siegel, on the other hand, made no secret of the fact that he was starstruck by Hollywood and sometimes wished that he too had become an actor. He viewed Raft as the Real McCoy in this arena and gave him due respect. Hoping to get ever closer to the Hollywood action, while at the same time expanding his "operations," Siegel moved to California in 1937.

Natural Born Actor?

In no time, Siegel was hobnobbing with major celebrities even as his deadly business dealings escalated. In 1941, Raft was shooting *Manpower* with the legendary Marlene Dietrich, when Siegel showed up on the set to observe. After watching Raft go through a few takes before heading off to his dressing room, Siegel told his buddy that he could do the scene better. An amused Raft told his friend to go ahead and give it a shot. Over the course of the next few minutes, the smirk would leave Raft's face.

Siegel reenacted Raft's scene perfectly. He had not only memorized the dialogue line for line, but he interpreted Raft's nuanced gestures as well. This was no small feat given the fact that Siegel had absolutely no training as an actor. A stunned Raft told Siegel that he just might have what it takes to be an actor.

A Dream Unfulfilled

But such Tinseltown dreams were not to be. Despite his demonstrated talent, moviemakers probably wouldn't have used him. And who could blame them? What if

Siegel decided to go "Bugsy" on them for not awarding him a role, for critiquing his performance, or for changing his lines? Temperamental actors are one thing; homicidal ones, quite another.

History shows that Siegel played it fast and loose from that point forward, putting most of his energies into creating the Flamingo Hotel and, along with it, the gaming capital of the world—Las Vegas. Siegel's mob associates from the East Coast put him in charge of construction of the opulent hotel. Siegel envisioned an extravagant hotel and, at least for him, money was no object. But when costs soared to $6 million—four times the original budget—Siegel's associates became concerned.

On June 20, 1947, Siegel's dreams of a life on the silver screen came to an abrupt end when a number of well-placed rounds from an M-1 Carbine sent the Hollywood gangster into the afterworld at age 41. It is believed that Siegel was killed by his own mob associates. They probably believed he was pilfering money from the organization. Siegel's life and grisly end are grand pieces of mob drama that got their due on the silver screen in the 1991 flick *Bugsy*, which starred Warren Beatty as the doomed mobster.

Craziest Coke Claims: Fact vs. Fiction

Coca-Cola has quickly become a staple of the all-American diet. It's also a regular in the rumor mill. For a common can of soda, you'd never guess all the strange things claimed about Coke. Most of the matters are no more than myth. A few, however, are the real thing.

Coke was originally green in color.

Afraid not. The kind folks at Coca-Cola say their bubbly beverage has been brown since the first bottle was produced in 1886. However, the glass was green in the early days, which may have led to the rumor.

Coke once contained cocaine.

Yep, this one is true: The original Coke formula used leaves from the coca plant. No one is entirely sure how much coke was in a bottle of coke, but some estimates place it at approximately two percent. Early ads even promoted the drink as a "brain tonic" that could cure headaches and chase away depression.

Once health experts began to realize the negative effects of cocaine, Coca-Cola modified its formula to use "de-cocainized" coca leaves that still have the same flavor—a process still used today. A company called Stepan has a factory where workers remove the cocaine from the leaves and ship the product to the Coca-Cola warehouse. Surgeons then use the leftover cocaine, which is legal as a local anesthetic for minor surgeries. Stepan is the only legal U.S. supplier of cocaine for these purposes.

Coke can be used as a household cleaner.

True—and your kitchen counter will never taste better. The company says the drink's acidic nature *could* hold the power to clean. Coke points out, however, that many other acidic agents—vinegar, for example—are considered completely safe as food ingredients. Coke notes that "rubbing something in a cloth soaked in a soft drink is not at all like drinking a soft drink" because "people don't hold soft drinks in their mouths for long periods of time." Also, Coke says, your saliva neutralizes the acid before it moves any lower in your body.

Coke will dissolve corrosion.

This statement also has some truth to it. Because of the acidic level mentioned above, the drink could theoretically knock some rust off of corroded metals. The Coca-Cola Company, however, recommends instead using a product actually designed for that purpose.

Coke gives you kidney stones.

False. Coke claims its product has never been shown to cause stones and may, in contrast, help prevent them. Not having enough liquid in your diet can contribute to the problem, and Coke, its reps say, provides a "pleasant and refreshing way to consume part of [your] daily fluid requirements." These people are good.

Coke works as a spermicide.

We hate to be the ones to break the news, but no. The myth started after the debut of New Coke in 1985, when scientists began to notice an increase in birth rates in parts of Africa. As the story goes, two Harvard researchers looked into it and found women in the villages had, in fact, been using the drink as a contraceptive. The scientists decided to test both New Coke and the original Coke to see what was going on. They found New Coke was five times less effective than original Coke as a spermicide, which explained the increased rate. Both drinks, though, had too mild an effect to be considered even remotely practical.

CHAPTER 4

MEDICAL MAYHEM

Unusual Medical Maladies

The human body is able to play some nasty tricks on its owner. While none of them are considered life-threatening, the six syndromes and disorders described below are documented cases of unusual medical maladies.

Who Is That?

Take the interesting and perplexing diagnosis of **Capgras Syndrome**, a rare psychological disorder that makes sufferers suspicious of their loved ones or even their own reflections. For a number of reasons, including schizophrenia, epilepsy, and malformed temporal lobes of the brain, Capgras victims have difficulty making physical and emotional connections with the people, places, and things they see, even ones that have been a part of their lives for years. Sufferers see themselves in a mirror or other shiny surfaces and wonder who the stranger is that's peering back at them. According to Dr. V. S. Ramachandran, director of the Center for Brain and Cognition at the University of California, San Diego, people diagnosed with this disorder can also find themselves suspicious of animals or other objects, such as a pair of running shoes. In such cases, they convince themselves that someone has broken into their home and replaced familiar objects with imposters.

Can You Direct Me to the Loo?

Foreign Accent Syndrome is even more rare: a disorder that causes the afflicted to suddenly and unexplainably speak in an unfamiliar dialect. One of the first cases of FAS was discovered in 1941 after a young Norwegian woman sustained a shrapnel injury to her head during a wartime air raid. Although she had never been out of her home country, she suddenly began speaking with a German accent, which resulted in her being shunned by her family and friends. In Indiana, a 57-year-old woman suffered a stroke in 1999 and began speaking with a British accent, including colloquialisms like "bloody" and "loo."

Get Your Hands Off of Me!

If there was ever a malady that a high school boy might envy, it's **Alien Hand Syndrome**, also known as **Dr. Strangelove Syndrome**. Alien Hand Syndrome is caused by damage to the parietal or occipital lobe of the brain. Those afflicted often find one of their hands operating independently from the rest of their body and sometimes completely against their conscious will. AHS sufferers often report incidences of a "rogue hand" getting involved in disobedient behavior such as undoing buttons or removing clothing. One patient reported a bizarre incident in which her right hand put a cigarette into her mouth. Before she could light it, her left hand yanked the cigarette out and crushed it in an ashtray.

Please Pass the Dirt

At one time or another all kids will experiment by eating an occasional handful of dirt. The good news is that it's a passing phase for the majority of youngsters. The bad news is that if this fascination with eating nonfood items persists longer than a month, your child could be afflicted with **Pica**. Associated with developmental disabilities such as autism or mental retardation, Pica typically affects children younger than 24 months. It can also appear in people with epilepsy and pregnant women.

Pica sufferers find themselves craving and consuming a wide variety of nonfood items such as dirt, sand, hair, glue, buttons, paint chips, plaster, laundry starch, cigarette butts, paper, soap, and even feces. There was even one documented case of "cutlery craving," in which a 47-year-old Englishman underwent more than 30 operations to remove various items from his stomach—including eight dinner forks.

Another form of Pica, called **Geophagia**, is practiced by cultures that eat earth substances such as dirt and clay to relieve nausea, morning sickness, diarrhea, and to remove toxins from their bodies.

Something Smells Fishy Around Here

Bad breath, body odor, and the occasional flatulence—we've all had to deal with them in one way or another. But how would you like to live with someone who constantly smelled of pungent fish? A rare metabolic disorder called **Fish Odor Syndrome** (also known as trimethylaminuria or TMAU) results in the afflicted releasing an enzyme called trimethylamine through their sweat, urine, and breath. This enzyme also happens to give off a strong "fishy" odor. The condition appears to be more common in women than men, and researchers suspect that female sex hormones such as estrogen or progesterone may be at fault.

While there is no cure for Fish Odor Syndrome, people afflicted can control the disease by avoiding eggs, certain meats, fish, legumes, and foods that contain choline, nitrogen, and sulfur. And, of course, showering regularly.

A Permanent Bad Hair Day

If you've suffered from the occasional bad hair day, consider yourself lucky—you could be afflicted with **Uncombable Hair Syndrome**. UHS is a rare disease that affects boys and girls before puberty. In fact, it's so rare that there have only been 60 cases reported in medical literature between 1973 and 1998.

UHS is an inherited disease with subtle hair changes noted in several preceding generations. It begins with a hair follicle that produces triangular hair shafts with several longitudinal grooves that also has very little pigment and is exceptionally dry and brittle. Because the hair is so dry, it rarely lies down; instead, the hair grows straight out from the scalp.

So what should you do if you are diagnosed with UHS? First, cancel your appointment with your hairdresser. People afflicted with UHS typically experience alopecia, or periodic baldness. The hair that does grow frequently breaks off before it has time to mature. And there is hope: There has been some success with medication, and some cases have recovered spontaneously several years after the first outbreak.

Medical Atrocities on Display at Philadelphia's Mütter Museum

Located at the College of Physicians of Philadelphia, the Mütter Museum is perhaps the most grotesque, or at least one of the most shockingly fascinating museums in the United States. Its collection of human skulls, preserved brains (eyes included), and freaks of nature will entertain those with even the most morbid curiosities.

It's also one of the most elegant museums open to the public, with red carpet, brass railings, and redwood-lined display cases. It might even appear a bit highbrow if the curators themselves didn't acknowledge what a uniquely abnormal exhibit they were pushing—a refreshing attitude evident in their motto "Disturbingly Informative."

The museum originated in 1859, when Dr. Thomas Mütter donated several thousand dollars and his personal collection of 1,700 medical specimens to the College of Physicians. Merging it with their own meager collection, the institution used Mütter's money to build new quarters to house it all and opened it to both students and the public.

Further acquisitions expanded the museum's collection tremendously, as doctors contributed specimens they'd acquired through their own private practices and studies. A large number of them have been skeletal, such as a woman's rib cage that became cartoonishly compressed by years of wearing tight corsets, and the 19th-century Peruvian skulls showing primitive trephinations (holes cut or drilled in the head). There are also the combined skeletons of infants born with a shared skull and the bones of a man suffering a condition in which superfluous bone grows in patches, eventually fusing the skeleton together and immobilizing it and its owner. Most popular, though, is the skeleton of a man measuring 7'6", the tallest of its kind on display in North America, which stands next to that of a 3'6" female dwarf.

Other items include heads sliced like loaves of bread, both front to back and side to side, and outdated medical instruments, many of which look torturous. Curators also have in their possession more than 2,000 objects removed from people's throats and airways, a vintage iron lung, and photographs of some of medicine's most bizarre human deformities.

The museum even has its own celebrities of sorts. For example, there's Madame Dimanche, an 82-year-old Parisian whose face and the drooping, ten-inch horn growing from her forehead have been preserved in lifelike wax. There's also the unidentified corpse of a woman known simply as the Soap Lady, whose body was unearthed in 1874. The particular composition of the soil in which she was buried transformed the fatty tissues in her body, essentially preserving her as a human-shape bar of soap. And who can forget Eng and Chang, the conjoined brothers who toured the world with P. T. Barnum and inspired the term "Siamese twins"? The Mütter Museum not only has a plaster cast of their torsos, but also their actual connected livers.

13 People with Extra Body Parts

Doctors call them supernumerary body parts, but here are a few people who always had a spare hand (or finger or head).

1. Anne Boleyn, second wife to Henry VIII of England, is commonly believed to have had 11 fingers and possibly a third breast. Historians believe that she did have a extra finger or at least some sort of growth on her hand that resembled an extra finger, but it is unlikely that she had an extra breast. This rumor may have been started by her enemies because in Tudor times an extra breast was believed to be the sign of a witch.

2. Major league baseball pitcher Antonio Alfonseca has six fingers on each hand, but he claims the extra fingers do not affect his pitching, as they do not usually touch the ball. In most cases of polydactylism (extra fingers or toes), the extra digit has only limited mobility, or cannot be moved at all, and is often surgically removed shortly after birth. The condition is reported in about one child in every 500.

3. Actor Mark Wahlberg has a third nipple on the left side of his chest. Early in his career, he considered having it removed, but he later came to accept it. Around 2 percent of women and slightly fewer men have a supernumerary nipple, although they are often mistaken for moles. They can be found anywhere between the armpit and groin, and range from a tiny lump (like Wahlberg's) to a small extra breast, sometimes even capable of lactation.

4. In 2006, a 24-year-old man from India checked himself into a New Delhi hospital and asked doctors to remove his extra penis so that he could marry and lead a normal sex life. To protect his privacy, doctors would not disclose his identity or that of the hospital but did confirm that the operation took place. The condition, known as diphallia or penile duplication, is extremely rare, with only around 100 cases ever officially documented.

5. In extremely rare cases, a baby may be born with a parasitic twin head. The extra head does not have a functioning brain, which is what differentiates this condition from that of conjoined twins. In effect, the baby is born with the head of its dead twin attached to its body. There have only ever been eight documented cases, and, of these, only three have survived birth. One of these was Rebeca Martinez, born in the Dominican Republic in December 2003, the first baby to undergo an operation to remove the second head. She died on February 7, 2004, after an 11-hour operation.

6. A similar condition is polycephaly, the condition of having more than one functioning head. There are many documented occurrences of this in the animal kingdom, although in most human cases we refer to the condition as conjoined twins. One recent case was that of Syafitri, born in Indonesia in 2006. These conjoined twins were given just one name by their parents who insisted that they were, in fact, one baby girl since they had only one heart and shared a body. It would have been impossible for doctors to separate the conjoined twins, and Syafitri died of unknown causes just two weeks after she was born.

7. Hermaphroditism—the condition of being born with both male and female reproductive organs—is more common than you might think, existing in some degree in around 1 percent of the population. In 1843, when Levi Suydam, a 23-year-old resident of Salisbury, Connecticut, wanted to vote for the Whig candidate in a local election, the opposition party objected, saying Suydam was really a woman and therefore did not have the right to vote. A doctor examined Suydam and declared that he had a penis and was therefore a man. He voted and the Whig candidate won by a single vote.

8. In 2006, a boy named Jie-Jie was born in China with two left arms. Although all three of his arms looked normal, neither left arm was fully functional, and, when he was two months old, doctors in Shanghai removed the one closest to his chest after tests revealed it was less developed.

9. While advances in medical technology mean that Jie Jie will go on to lead a relatively normal life, Francesco Lentini, who was born in Sicily in 1889, had a life that was anything but. He was born with three legs, two sets of genitals, and an extra foot growing from the knee of his third leg—the remains of a conjoined twin that had died in the womb. Rejected by his parents, he was raised by an aunt, then in a home for disabled children before moving to America when he was eight. He became "The Great Lentini" and toured with major circus and sideshow acts, including the Ringling Brothers' Circus and Barnum and Bailey. Part of his act included using his third leg to kick a soccer ball across the stage. He married, raised four children, and lived longer than any other three-legged person, dying in Florida in 1966 at age 78.

10. Josephene Myrtle Corbin, born in 1868, could see Lentini his three legs and raise him one. She was a dipygus, meaning that she had two separate pelvises and four legs. As with Lentini, these were the residual parts of a conjoined twin. She could move all of the legs, but they were too weak to walk on. Like Lentini, she was a great success in sideshows with the stage name "The Four-Legged Girl from Texas." She married a doctor with whom she had five children. Legend has it that three of her children were born from one pelvis, and two from the other.

11. Born in 1932 to a poor farming family in Georgia, Betty Lou Williams was the youngest of 12 children. Doctors claimed she was a healthy child . . . except for the two extra arms and legs emerging from the side of her body. From the age of two, Williams worked for *Ripley's Believe It Or Not* and earned quite a living on the sideshow circuit—she put her siblings through college and bought her parents a large farm. She grew up to be a lovely and generous young lady, but when she was jilted by her fiance at age 23, she died from an asthma attack exacerbated by the head of the parasitic twin lodged in her abdomen.

12. Another sideshow star of the early 20th century was Jean Libbera, "The Man with Two Bodies," who was born in Rome in 1884. Libbera was born with a parasitic conjoined twin attached to his front. Photos of Libbera show a shrunken body, about 18 inches long, emerging from his abdomen with its head a parently embedded inside. He died in 1934, at age 50.

13. It might seem unusual for a woman to have two uteruses, but the condition known as uterine didelphys occurs in about one in 1,000 women. In fact, Hannah Kersey, her mother, and her sister all have two wombs. But Hannah made history in 2006 when she gave birth to triplets—a set of identical twin girls from one womb and a third, fraternal sister from the other womb. There have been about 70 known pregnancies in separate wombs in the past 100 years, but the case of triplets is the first of its kind and doctors estimate the likelihood is about one in 25 million.

The Story of Anesthesia

In the middle of the 19th century, three intoxicating solvents with bad reputations became the first crude "switches" that could turn consciousness off and on—paving the way for the revolution of painless surgical medicine.

On March 30, 1842, a doctor from rural Georgia laid an ether-soaked towel across the mouth and nose of a young patient with two cysts on the back of his neck. The physician, Crawford Williamson Long, excised one of the growths while his patient was under. In the process, he made medical and scientific history. Long was perhaps the first doctor to use what is today called a "general anesthetic"—a substance that reduces or eliminates conscious awareness in a patient, allowing a doctor to perform incisions, sutures, and all other surgical procedures in between.

The "general"—which means complete or near-complete unconsciousness—is quite different from the targeted "local" anesthetic, an invention with origins shrouded in mystery. (Some ancient Inca trepanation rituals involved drilling a hole in the patient's skull to allow evil spirits to escape; to reduce the literally mind-numbing pain, the Incan shaman chewed leaves of the narcotic coca plant and spat the paste into the subject's wound.)

Unfortunately for Georgia's Dr. Long, the awards and acclaim that should have accompanied his medical milestone went to a dentist from Boston, who used ether four years later to knock out a patient in order to remove a tooth. Because this procedure was performed at the world-renowned Massachusetts General Hospital—and not at a backwoods country practice in the Deep South—the fame of the Massachusetts innovator, William T. G. Morton, was practically assured. Within two months of Morton's tooth extraction, doctors across Europe were toasting the Yankee who had invented pain-free surgery.

The story of the stolen spotlight, however, can't entirely be blamed on the prejudice of urban versus rural or North versus South. Long, who was known to enjoy the occasional "ether frolic," didn't publicize his use of ether as a general anesthetic until 1849, seven years after his initial use of it, and three years after Morton's world-acclaimed surgery.

Wake up, Mr. Green. Mr. Green?

By 1849, a London physician, John Snow, had invented a specialized ether inhaler to better administer a safe but effective dose of the painless surgical gas. Snow was responding to the need for more scientific care in the fledgling field of anesthesiology. Lethal doses of ether had already been administered in some botched surgeries, and Snow eventually championed chloroform, which, he would later write, is "almost impossible . . . [to cause] a death . . . in the hands of a medical man who is applying it with ordinary intelligence and attention."

Chloroform and ether each had their downsides, though. Chloroform could damage the liver and even cause cardiac arrest, but ether required more time for the patient to both enter and exit the anesthetized state.

Nothing To Laugh About

Some American practitioners championed a third popular early anesthetic: nitrous oxide or "laughing gas," although its reputation suffered when not enough of it was administered in an early demonstration during a tooth extraction at Harvard Medical School. When the patient cried out in pain, the dentist, Horace Wells, was booed out of the room. In a turn of tragic irony, Wells later became a chloroform addict and committed suicide in 1848, just three years after the Harvard fiasco.

By the 1860s and '70s, many surgeons had given up advocating one gas over another, preferring instead to use a mixture—either chloroform or nitrous oxide to induce anesthesia, followed by ether to keep the patient in an unconscious state.

The Lobotomy: A Sordid History

There's a reason why lobotomies have taken a place next to leeches in the Health Care Hall of Shame.

Beyond Hollywood

Few people have firsthand experience with lobotomized patients. For many of us, any contact with these convalescents comes via Hollywood—that searing image at the end of One Flew Over the Cuckoo's Nest of Jack Nicholson, as Randle Patrick McMurphy, lying comatose. Hopefully, we've all experienced enough to know that Hollywood doesn't always tell it like it is. What would be the point of a medical procedure that turns the patient into a vegetable? Then again, even if Hollywood is prone to exaggeration, the fact is that a lobotomy is a pretty terrible thing.

Dissecting the Lobotomy

What exactly is a lobotomy? Simply put, it's a surgical procedure that severs the paths of communication between the prefrontal lobe and the rest of the brain. This prefrontal lobe—the part of the brain closest to the forehead—is a structure that appears to have great influence on personality and initiative. So the obvious question is: Who the heck thought it would be a good idea to disconnect it?

It started in 1890, when German researcher Friederich Golz removed portions of his dog's brain. He noticed afterward that the dog was slightly more mellow—and the lobotomy was born. The first lobotomies performed on humans took place in Switzerland two years later.

The six patients who were chosen all suffered from schizophrenia, and while some did show post-op improvement, two others died. Apparently this was a time in medicine when an experimental procedure that killed 33 percent of its subjects was considered a success. Despite these grisly results, lobotomies became more commonplace, and one early proponent of the surgery even received a Nobel Prize.

The most notorious practitioner of the lobotomy was American physician Walter Freeman, who performed the procedure on more than three thousand patients—including Rosemary Kennedy, the sister of President John F. Kennedy—from the 1930s to the 1960s.

Freeman pioneered a surgical method in which a metal rod (known colloquially as an "ice pick") was inserted into the eye socket, driven up into the brain, and hammered home. This is known as a transorbital lobotomy.

Freeman and other doctors in the United States lobotomized an estimated 40,000 patients before an ethical outcry over the procedure prevailed in the 1950s. Although the mortality rate had improved since the early trials, it turned out that the ratio of success to failure was not much higher: A third of the patients got better, a third stayed the same, and a third became much worse. The practice had generally ceased in the United States by the early 1970s, and it is now illegal in some states.

Who Got Them?

Lobotomies were performed only on patients with extreme psychological impairments, after no other treatment proved to be successful. The frontal lobe of the brain is involved in reasoning, emotion, and personality, and disconnecting it can have a powerful effect on a person's behavior. Unfortunately, the changes that a lobotomy causes are unpredictable and often negative. Today, there are far more precise and far less destructive manners of affecting the brain through antipsychotic drugs and other pharmaceuticals.

So it's not beyond the realm of possibility that Nicholson's character in *Cuckoo's Nest* could become zombie-like. If the movie gets anything wrong, it's that a person as highly functioning as McMurphy probably wouldn't have been recommended for a lobotomy. The vindictive Nurse Ratched is the one who makes the call, which raises a fundamental moral question: Who is qualified to decide whether someone should have a lobotomy?

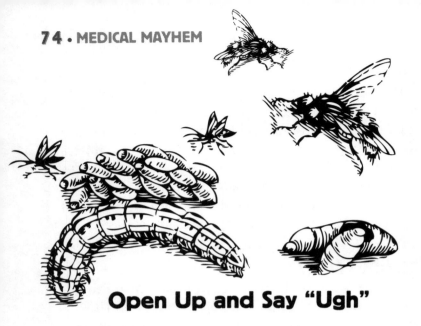

Open Up and Say "Ugh"

One of the last things a patient wants to see as they look across a sterile operating room are leeches, maggots, and scum-sucking fish. But all three have earned a solid place in the medical community—simply by doing what comes naturally.

The Flies Have It

Maggots are nothing more than fly larvae—one of the most basic forms of life. But to many patients with wounds that refuse to respond to conventional treatment, they are a godsend. For the majority of people recovering from life-threatening wounds, contusions, and limb reattachments, antibiotics provide much of the follow-up care they need. But for a small percentage of patients who do not respond to modern medicines, maggots slither in to fill the gap.

Applied to a dressing that is made in the form of a small "cage," maggots are applied to almost any area that does not respond well to conventional treatment. The bug thrives on consuming dead tissue (a process called "debridement"), while ignoring the healthy areas. After several days, the maggots are removed—but only after they have consumed up to ten times their own weight in dead tissue, cleaned the wound, and left an ammonia-like antimicrobial enzyme behind.

While maggot therapy may not be everyone's cup of tea, it is effective in treating diseases like diabetes where restricting circulation for any reason can often result in nerve damage and even loss of limb.

Golden Age of Leeches

Similar to the maggot, leeches are small animal organisms that have been used by physicians and barbers (who, in the olden days, were also considered surgeons) for over 2,500 years for treating everything from headaches and mental illnesses to—gulp—hemorrhoids. And while they might appear to be on the low end of the evolution scale, leeches actually have 32 brains!

Leeches are raised commercially around the world with the majority coming from France, Hungary, Ukraine, Romania, Egypt, Algeria, Turkey, and the United States. Used extensively until the 19th century, the "Golden Age of Leeches" was usurped by the adoption of modern concepts of pathology and microbiology. *Hirudotherapy*, or the medicinal use of leeches, has enjoyed a recent resurgence after their demonstrated ability to heal patients when other means have failed.

Leeches feed on the blood of humans and other animals by piercing the skin with a long proboscis. Oftentimes this is the most effective way to drain a postsurgical area

of blood, and it can actually facilitate the healing process.
At the same time leeches attach to their host, they inject
a blood-thinning anticoagulant; they continue until they
have consumed up to five times their body weight in
blood. The host rarely feels the bite because the leech
also injects a local anesthetic before it pierces the skin.

The Doctor (Fish) Is In

Another unlikely ally to the medical community is the
doctor fish, found in bathing pools in the small Turkish
town of Kangal. The therapeutic pools in Kangal are a
popular destination for people suffering from fractures,
joint traumas, gynecological maladies, and skin diseases.
While the pools themselves have a number of beneficial
qualities such as the presence of selenium (a mineral
that protects against free radicals and helps with wound
healing), they are most famous for the doctor fish that
live there.

At only 15 to 20 centimeters in length, doctor fish are
relatively small and do not physically attach themselves
to their host like leeches or maggots. Instead, they sur-
round a person's skin, striking and licking it. They are
particularly fond of eating psoriatic plaque and other
skin diseases that have been softened by the water, eating
only the dead and hyper-keratinized tissue while leaving
the healthy tissue behind.

While many people might be uncomfortable at the
thought of being surrounded by a school of fish feasting
on their skin, many actually enjoy the pleasant and relaxing sensation of getting a "micro-massage."

Heads Up: The Study of Phrenology

Sure, someone may look like a nice enough guy, but a phrenologist might just diagnose the same fella as a potential axe murderer.

He Had the Gall

There are bumps in the road and bumps in life. Then there are the bumps on our heads. In the last half of the 19th century, the bumps and lumps and shapes of the human skull became an area of scientific study known as *phrenology*.

Early in the century, an Austrian physicist named Franz Joseph Gall theorized that the shape of the head followed the shape of the brain. Moreover, he wrote, the skull's shape was determined by the development of the brain's various parts. He described 27 separate parts of the brain and attributed to each one specific personality traits.

Gall's phrenological theories reached the public at a time of widespread optimism in Europe and North America. New and startling inventions seemed to appear every week. No problem was insurmountable, no hope unattainable. Physical science prevailed. By mid-century, Gall's theories had spread favorably throughout industrialized society. What was particularly attractive about phrenology was its value as both an indicator and predictor of psychological traits. If these traits could be identified—and phrenology presumably could do this—they could be re-engineered through "moral counseling" before they became entrenched as bad habits, which could result in socially unacceptable behavior. On the other hand, latent goodness, intellect, and rectitude could also be identified and nurtured.

As it grew in popularity, phrenology found its way into literature as diverse as the Brontë family's writings and those of Edgar Allen Poe. It influenced the work of philosopher William James. Poet Walt Whitman was so proud of his phrenological chart that he published it five times. Thomas Edison was also a vocal supporter. "I never knew I had an inventive talent until phrenology told me so," he said. "I was a stranger to myself until then."

Criminal Minds

Early criminologists such as Cesare Lombroso and Èmile Durkheim (the latter considered to be the founder of the academic discipline of sociology) saw remarkable possibilities for phrenology's use in the study of criminal behavior. Indeed, according to one tale, the legendary Old West figure Bat Masterson invited a phrenologist to Dodge City to identify horse thieves and cattle rustlers. A lecture before an audience of gun-toting citizenry ended with the audience shooting out the lights and the lecturer hastily departing through the back exit.

In 1847, Orson Fowler, a leading American phrenologist, conducted an analysis of a Massachusetts wool trader and found him "to go the whole figure or nothing," a man who would "often find (his) motives are not understood." Sure enough, years later Fowler was proven to be on the money. The man was noted slavery abolitionist John Brown, and he definitely went the "whole figure."

Bumpology Booms

By the turn of the century, the famous and not so famous were flocking to have their skulls analyzed. Phrenology had become a fad and, like all fads, it attracted a number of charlatans. Death masks and cranial molds also became popular sideshow exhibits. By the 1920s, the science had degenerated into a parlor game. Disrepute and discredit followed, but not before new expressions slipped into the language. Among these: "low brow" and "high brow" describe varying intellectual capacity, as well as the offhand remark, "You should have your head examined."

Nevertheless, phrenology did figure in the initial development of American psychiatry, and it helped point medical scientists in new directions: neurology for one and, more recently, genomics—the study of the human genome.

CHAPTER 5

THE THING ABOUT HUMANS IS . . .

It's No Myth:
A Human Voice Can Shatter Glass

You're not likely to do it accidentally, even if you do spend a lot of time yelling at your tableware, but it's definitely possible.

Air, Space, and Sound

First, a few words about air, space, and sound. The word "air" probably makes you think of nothingness—empty space. But the air we breathe is actually a fluid—a gas— in which we are immersed. And the sounds that we hear are actually vibrations that travel through this fluid like waves.

Your vocal cords are machines for creating these waves. When you speak, sing, freestyle beat-box, etc., air from your lungs rushes past your vocal cords, and those two taut membranes vibrate. First, the outrushing air makes your vocal cords flex outward, pushing out a wave of increased air pressure; then they rebound inward, creating a wave of decreasing air pressure.

When your vocal cords vibrate, they're moving in and out incredibly quickly to create waves of air pressure fluctuation, or sound. The sound's pitch is determined in part by how rapidly your vocal cords are vibrating—in other words, the *frequency* of the air pressure fluctuation. The sound's volume is determined by the force of each fluctuation, or the wave's amplitude.

Sound waves travel through the fluid air and vibrate against and within anything that they encounter. For example, sound waves rapidly move your eardrums back and forth, which is how you hear. And if a sound is loud enough, its waves can have other effects. If you've ever been at a stop light behind a car with a booming audio system in the back, you may have noticed that the car's trunk looks like it's shuddering under the assault of those powerful sound waves. But the auditory assault of even the loudest stereo isn't enough to break the car's windows, so how can the sound waves of a mere human voice shatter glass?

It has to do with frequency and resonance. The structure and composition of an object determine exactly how it will vibrate—this is known as its natural frequency. Think of a tuning fork that vibrates in just the right way to make a particular note, no matter how you hit it. You get an extra vibration boost—a resonant sound wave—when you produce a sound wave with a frequency that lines up with the object's natural vibration frequency. It's like pushing a kid on a swing—when he's moving away from you, you push him to add an extra boost. Every time you do this, the arc of the swing increases, and the kid reaches higher and higher.

In the same way, just when an object is already vibrating to the left, the resonant sound wave pushes it to the left; just when it's vibrating to the right, the resonant sound wave pushes it to the right. The amplitude steadily increases, and the object vibrates more rapidly. A crystal glass has above-average natural resonance and is fragile, so the right tone can create enough vibration to shatter it.

Technique Is Everything

To break a glass with your voice, you have to do two things:

1. Hit the note that has the strongest resonant frequency for the glass. This is called the fundamental frequency, or the natural frequency mentioned earlier.

2. Produce a sound with enough amplitude to vibrate the glass violently. In other words, you have to be loud.

An untrained singer can accomplish this with an amplifier providing a boost. But you need a skilled singer with strong lungs to do it unassisted. Many have claimed success, but there wasn't conclusive proof until a 2005 *MythBusters* episode showed rock singer Jaime Vendera accomplishing the feat—after twenty attempts. Don't let that guy near your Waterford Crystal collection.

Getting a Charge Out of Life

It may seem odd to compare the human body to an electric power generator, but rare cases around the world have shown that some people are born with shocking abilities . . . literally. Jacqueline Priestman, a British woman, consistently produces ten times the static electricity of a normal human being.

How to "Conduct" Oneself

Priestman, who ironically married an electrician before she knew about her strange ability, grew up with no more than the usual mild electromagnetic field that surrounds every human. But when she turned 22, sparks began to fly. Priestman noticed that her mere touch would cause ordinary household appliances to short out and fizzle, while others could use the same appliances with no problem. She could also change the channels on her TV by going near it.

Priestman has had to buy at least 30 new vacuum cleaners in her married life, plus five irons and several washing machines. Michael Shallis, a lecturer at Oxford University and a former astrophysicist, studied Priestman and told a British newspaper in 1985 that she was actually able to transmit tiny bolts of "lightning" that could affect any electrical system nearby. He had no explanation for the phenomenon but did say that most similar cases he had investigated involved women. For example, Pauline Shaw flooded her house every time she tried to do laundry because the washing machine fuses would blow when she touched the dials. The washer's door would then pop open and turn the machine into a fountain.

For more than four years, Shallis studied 600 people with Priestman's condition and, eventually, wrote a book about them called *The Electric Connection*.

SLI-ding Through Life

There is a name for those like Priestman and Shaw. Because people with abnormal amounts of static electricity often cause streetlights to flicker when they pass by, scientists call the strange disorder Street Light Interference, or SLI. People with the condition are called SLI-ders, or Sliders.

An older name for the phenomenon is High Voltage Syndrome, or HVS. Around 1930, one HVS patient, Count John Berenyi of Hungary, was reportedly able to make neon light tubes glow merely by holding them. And according to author Vincent Gaddis, the National Safety Council investigates what he calls "human spark plugs"—people who can start fires with the electrical abundance of their mere presence. One woman made a rather poor vocational choice in the early 1940s when she got a job gluing shoes together with rubber cement, a highly flammable substance. She allegedly started at least five fires in the factory and could ignite a pail of rubber cement merely by standing near it. She had to quit after suffering severe burns in one of the fires.

Even babies can act as superconductors. In 1869, a child born in France was so highly charged that anyone who approached him received a sharp electric shock. He even exhibited a faint glow around his hands. The infant died from undetermined causes when he was only nine months old, and, according to witnesses, his entire body radiated light at the time of his passing.

Radiant Blood

The strange baby was not the only human known to glow. Luminous people have been reported in many circumstances, and their abilities are often tied to medical conditions. Anna Monaro, an Italian woman, gained attention in 1934, when her breasts began to spontaneously emit blue phosphorescent light while she was sleeping. The weird condition lasted for weeks and drew many eminent doctors and scientists to study her firsthand. They were even able to capture the glow on film. Many theories were offered, from "electrical and magnetic organisms in the woman's body" to "radiant blood." Eventually, the bizarre condition went away and did not return.

Through No Fault of Her Own

A Welsh woman named Mary Jones set off a religious fervor in 1905, when amazing forms of light appeared to emit from her body. Jones had already gained some notoriety as a local preacher when people began to observe glowing, exploding balls of lightning and electric-blue rectangles hovering near her as she spoke. The light show lasted for several months and attracted hundreds of believers, along with a cadre of scientific observers. Various explanations were offered for the lights, from a misidentification of the planet Venus to fault lines under the chapel where Jones preached. Scientists speculated that movements of the earth had stressed the bedrock, issuing gases that resulted in geomagnetic anomalies in the air above.

Lightning Reactions

Not everyone with an electric attraction finds the sensation enjoyable. Grace Charlesworth, a woman from the UK, had lived in a house for almost 40 years when, in 1968, she began receiving unexplainable shocks both indoors and out. The weird voltage was strong enough to spin Charlesworth's body in a complete circle, and at times, it would even make her head shake uncontrollably. The voltage was sometimes visible as sparks, and she could escape only by leaving her house or yard, as she was never bothered elsewhere.

Charlesworth blamed her problem on the noise from a compressor in a nearby factory, but fixing the compressor did not stop the mysterious electricity. One possible contributing factor was that the house had been hit by lightning five times. Some people become so sensitive to electrical currents that they cannot even live in homes with any sort of wiring or appliances. An Irish woman named Margaret Cousins had to move to a cabin with no utilities in 1996 because her condition had become so painful. But two years later she had to move again after two cell phone towers were installed nearby and caused her pain to return.

16 Unusual Facts about the Human Body

1. Don't stick out your tongue if you want to hide your identity. Similar to fingerprints, everyone also has a unique tongue print!

2. Your pet isn't the only one in the house with a shedding problem. Humans shed about 600,000 particles of skin every hour. That works out to about 1.5 pounds each year, so the average person will lose around 105 pounds of skin by age 70.

3. An adult has fewer bones than a baby. We start off life with 350 bones, but because bones fuse together during growth, we end up with only 206 as adults.

4. Did you know that you get a new stomach lining every three to four days? If you didn't, the strong acids your stomach uses to digest food would also digest your stomach.

5. Your nose is not as sensitive as a dog's, but it can remember 50,000 different scents.

6. The small intestine is about four times as long as the average adult is tall. If it weren't looped back and forth upon itself, its length of 18 to 23 feet wouldn't fit into the abdominal cavity, making things rather messy.

7. This will really make your skin crawl: Every square inch of skin on the human body has about 32 million bacteria on it, but fortunately, the vast majority of them are harmless.

8. The source of smelly feet, like smelly armpits, is sweat. And people sweat buckets from their feet. Your feet have 500,000 sweat glands and can produce more than a pint of sweat a day.

9. The air from a human sneeze can travel at speeds of 100 miles per hour or more—another good reason to cover your nose and mouth when you sneeze—or duck when you hear one coming your way.

10. Blood has a long road to travel: Laid end to end, there are about 60,000 miles of blood vessels in the human body. And the hard-working heart pumps about 2,000 gallons of blood through those vessels every day.

11. You may not want to swim in your spit, but if you saved it all up, you could. In a lifetime, the average person produces about 25,000 quarts of saliva enough to fill two swimming pools!

12. By 60 years of age, 60 percent of men and 40 percent of women will snore. But the sound of a snore can seem deafening. While snores average around 60 decibels, the noise level of normal speech, they can reach more than 80 decibels. Eighty decibels is as loud as the sound of a pneumatic drill breaking up concrete. Noise levels over 85 decibels are considered hazardous to the human ear.

13. Blondes may or may not have more fun, but they definitely have more hair. Hair color helps determine how dense the hair on your head is, and blondes (only natural ones, of course), top the list. The average human head has 100,000 hair follicles, each of which is capable of producing 20 individual hairs during a person's lifetime. Blondes average 146,000 follicles. People with black hair tend to have about 110,000 follicles, while those with brown hair are right on target with 100,000 follicles. Redheads have the least dense hair, averaging about 86,000 follicles.

14. If you're clipping your fingernails more often than your toenails, that's only natural. The nails that get the most exposure and are used most frequently grow the fastest. Fingernails grow fastest on the hand that you write with and on the longest fingers. On average, nails grow about one-tenth of an inch each month.

15. No wonder babies have such a hard time holding up their heads: The human head is one-quarter of our total length at birth but only one-eighth of our total length by the time we reach adulthood.

16. If you say that you're dying to get a good night's sleep, you could mean that literally. You can go without eating for weeks without succumbing, but ten days is tops for going without sleep. After ten days, you'll be asleep—forever!

Beauty Is Pain

For thousands of years, human beings (especially women) have tried to change or improve their appearance by applying cosmetics—sometimes with deadly results.

Back Then

In the old world, limited scientific knowledge prevented awareness that many toxic and lethal chemicals were constantly being coated on people's skin in the name of good looks. In fact, during the second millennium BC, Old Kingdom Egyptians took makeup so seriously that they invented the science of chemistry to produce it. Chemists at France's Louvre Museum and those of a leading cosmetics manufacturer recently analyzed ancient stores of kohl, or *mesdemet*, a darkening agent (black, or less commonly, green) that Egyptians applied to both upper and lower eyelids to protect vision from the glaring sun. (Not incidentally, kohl also created a smolderingly sexy, "smoky" eye.) The scientists found that kohl contained a dark sulfide of lead extracted from a mine near the Red Sea, as well as some synthetic compounds and 7–10 percent animal fat to make the mixture creamy—the same percentage manufacturers use to this day, although modern cosmetics usually contain vegetable fat.

Cleopatra and her contemporaries also wore "lipstick" made of carmine, obtained from crushed beetles, in a base made from ant's eggs. Ancient Egyptians and Romans used other cosmetics containing mercury and white lead. Tattoos? Those are nothing new to either the Egyptians or the Indians. For centuries, they have used the reddish vegetable dye henna to create temporary tattoo patterns on the skin and to color hair, as well. Like the Egyptians, Hindu culture also used kohl as eye makeup.

Pale Beauty

Women in Roman Britain used a tin-oxide cream to whiten their faces. In 1558, Queen Elizabeth I began a fad by doing the same with egg whites, vinegar, and white powdered lead, a deadly mixture that caused poisoning and, ironically, scarring. By the 1700s, black "beauty spot" patches to cover the scars became necessary accessories.

As a matter of fact, throughout Europe during the Middle Ages, the Renaissance, and up to the Industrial Revolution, having darker skin was considered a working-class no-no; light skin meant luxury because you could afford to stay inside. Therefore, upper-class people and upper-class wannabes lightened their skin—using white lead that often contained arsenic. In the 1800s, whitening the face was still one of the most common cosmetic practices. A mix of carbonate, hydroxide, and lead oxide was the norm. Unfortunately, when used repeatedly, this mixture could result in muscle paralysis or death.

And Now?

Of course, in modern times, we've learned our lesson. Or have we? In today's nail polishes, the reproductive toxin dibutyl phthalate, known as DBP, is a common ingredient. Other ingredients in nail polishes include formaldehyde (a carcinogen) and toluene, which has been linked to birth defects.

In 1992, an epidemic of papular and follicular rashes broke out in Switzerland, caused by vitamin E linoleate in a new line of cosmetics. In 2000, an outbreak of skin boils infected hundreds of pedicure customers in a California salon. Most recently, phthalates have hit the radar. Phthalates are a class of chemicals added to many consumer products, notably cosmetics and scented substances such as perfumes, soaps, and lotions. Some research, however, shows that phthalates have the unfortunate distinction of causing cancer, birth defects, and sexual dysfunction.

In autumn 2007, runway shows by designers from Versace to Vuitton featured a revival of the "Cleopatra" eye made famous by Elizabeth Taylor in the 1963 biopic. At the same time, the covers of various fashion magazines featured pale skin and deeply reddened lips—none of which, fortunately, are necessarily "to die for" anymore. It seems that humanity really takes the phrase "beauty is pain" to heart.

Old Age's Unwanted Growth Spurt

The older we get, the prettier we ain't. In addition to the sagging and the wrinkles, an ignominious side effect of aging is the dense thickets of hair that erupt from the ears, nose, and just about anywhere else you don't want them.

While you have no choice but to accept the grim destiny of old age, you can at least know what cruel twist of anatomical fate produces the hair-growth-in-the-wrong-places phenomenon. Whether you are a man or woman, the culprit appears to be female hormones. And take notice of the word "appears." You should know up front that afflictions such as cancer and diabetes, not excessive nose hair, are what tend to get most of the medical attention and research funding. Consequently, the explanation that follows is mostly conjecture.

Both men and women produce female hormones such as estrogen. These hormones restrict the growth of body hair and counteract male-type hormones such as testosterone (which are also present in both men and women), which trigger the growth of body hair. When you're younger, the male and female hormones maintain the balance they should. As you get older, production of the female hormones slows down. In other words, the male–female hormonal balance gets out of whack, and you begin to look like a Yeti. But it isn't all doom and gloom for old-timers: They get cheap movie tickets and can force people to sit through their long, rambling stories.

The Mummy Still Lives

The ancient Egyptians would be happy to know that 5,000 years later, mummification is still around. The processes have changed over the centuries, but if you want your corpse preserved like King Tut's was, you definitely have options.

How to Make a Mummy

Mummification simply means keeping some soft tissue—such as skin or muscle—around long after death. To create a mummy, you just need to keep the tissue from being eaten. Shooing vultures and cannibals away is simple enough, but keeping hungry bacteria at bay is no small feat. The trick is to make the body inhospitable to bacteria. Bacteria like it hot and wet, so mummification depends on keeping a body extremely cold and/or dry. The ancient Egyptians removed the corpse's internal organs, filled the cavity with linen pads, sprinkled the body with a drying compound called natron, and then wrapped it in bandages. In 1994, Egyptology professor Bob Brier successfully replicated this process—but most other modern mummy-makers use other means.

When Vladimir Lenin croaked in 1924, the Russians decided to mummify him. Their secret process involved immersing the corpse in a chemical bath that replaces all water. The results are impressive—Lenin today looks like Lenin on his deathbed. In 1952, the Argentineans took a similar tack with Eva Peron, the wife of dictator Juan Peron. They replaced bodily fluids with wax, making a wax dummy corpse.

Since 1967, dozens of people have opted for cryonics, a form of mummification in which doctors replace the water in the body with chemicals, and keep the deceased at a crisp –320 degrees Fahrenheit—at least until scientists figure out how to cure death.

Summum Mummies

The religious organization Summum also offers mummification, but without future reanimation in mind. First, the embalmers immerse the body in a chemical solution for 30 to 60 days to dissolve the water in the body. Next, they wrap the body in gauze and apply a layer of polyurethane, followed by a layer of fiberglass and resin. The body is then sealed in a bronze or stainless steel mummiform capsule.

Summun has a growing list of (still-living) human clients. The organization asks for a donation to cover its services, usually $67,000 for the process—not including the mummiform.

A Near-Perfect Mummy

The most impressive modern mummies come from a process called Plastination. First, embalmers pump a substance that halts decay into the corpse. Then, they remove the skin and other tissues, and immerse the body in an acetone solution, which dissolves the water and fats. Next, they immerse the body in liquid plastic inside a vacuum chamber and drop the pressure until the all the acetone boils and evaporates. The resulting vacuum in the body sucks in the plastic so that it permeates every nook and cranny. Before the liquid solidifies into hard plastic, embalmers pose the body. The result is a clean, educational sculpture, which also happens to be an actual corpse.

German anatomist Gunther von Hagens invented Plastination in 1977, and he's signed up in the neighborhood of 8,000 body donors—many of whom are now mummies in the traveling Body Worlds exhibition. It's completely free to sign up, so if you're looking to stick around after you pass on and you don't mind posing with tourists for the next few thousand years, the value is hard to beat.

If These Bones Could Talk

Early in the 20th century, archaeologists searched for the "missing link"—a fossil that would bridge the gap between apes and man. What was found, however, made monkeys out of everyone involved.

Fossil Facts or Fiction?

In November 1912, a story appeared in the English newspaper *Manchester Guardian*: Skull fragments had been found that could be of the utmost significance. "There seems to be no doubt whatever of its genuineness," wrote the reporter, characterizing the bones as perhaps "the oldest remnant of a human frame yet discovered on this planet." The story generated feverish speculation. On the night of December 18, 1912, a crowd jammed into the meeting of the Geological Society of London to learn about this amazing discovery. What they heard was that solicitor and amateur archeologist Charles Dawson had discovered two skull fragments and a jawbone from a gravel bed near Piltdown Common in East Sussex. He had been interested in this area ever since workmen, knowing of his archeological interest, had given him some interesting bone fragments from the pit several years before. Dawson had since been making his own excavations of the pit, aided by Arthur Smith Woodward, keeper of the Department of Geology at the British Museum.

The skull fragments were definitely human, but the jawbone was similar to an ape. If they came from the same creature, as Woodward and Dawson both hypothesized, then they had discovered the missing evolutionary link between ape and man. Woodward announced, "I therefore propose that the Piltdown specimen be regarded as a new type of genus of the family *Hominidae*."

A Deep Divide

Almost immediately, two distinct camps were formed: doubters and supporters. In Woodward's favor were the facts that the remains were found close together, that they were similar in color and mineralization, and that the teeth were worn down in a flat, human way—unlike those of an ape. Doubters contended the jawbone and skull fragments were too dissimilar to be from the same creature. American and French scientists tended to be skeptical, while the British generally accepted the validity of the discovery.

Woodward's side scored valuable points when a canine tooth missing from the Piltdown jaw was discovered in 1913 close to where the jawbone originally had been found. Hard on the heels of that find came another—an elephant bone that had been rendered into some type of tool and supposed to have been used by Piltdown Man.

In 1915, there came perhaps the most conclusive evidence of all: Dawson found the remains of a similar creature a scant two miles away from the site of the first discovery.

Bone Betrayal

So Piltdown Man entered the archaeological record. After Dawson died on August 10, 1916, no significant new Piltdown discoveries were made, but no matter. Even when a few scientists identified the jaw as that from an ape, they were ignored. However, as other fossil discoveries were made in subsequent years, it became evident that something wasn't quite right about Piltdown Man. Things really began unraveling in 1949, when a new dating technique called the fluorine absorption test was used on Piltdown Man. It revealed that the skull fragments were relatively modern and the jawbone was just a few decades old. Finally, in 1953 a group of scientists proved conclusively that Piltdown Man was a hoax. The jawbone had been stained to look old, the teeth filed down, and the bones placed at the site.

Although the identity of the Piltdown Man hoaxer has never been revealed—even Sir Arthur Conan Doyle, author of the Sherlock Holmes series of mysteries, is considered a suspect by some—most suspicion falls on Dawson, who was later found to have been involved in other archeological frauds. Ultimately, it seems that if seeing is believing, then Piltdown Man is proof that people will only see what they want to believe.

CHAPTER 6

HISTORICALLY SPEAKING

Millions of Mummies

It sounds like the premise of a horror movie—millions of excess mummies just piling up. But for the Egyptians, this was simply an excuse to get a little creative. The ancient Egyptians took death seriously. Their culture believed that the afterlife was a dark and tumultuous place where departed souls needed protection throughout eternity. By preserving their bodies as mummies, Egyptians provided their souls with a resting place—without which they would wander the afterlife forever.

Starting roughly around 3000 BC, Egyptian morticians began making a healthy business on the mummy trade. On receiving a corpse, they would first remove the brain and internal organs and store them in canopic jars. Next, they would stuff the body with straw to maintain its shape, cover it in salt and oils to preserve it from rotting, and then wrap it in linens—a process that could take up to 70 days. Finally, the finished mummies would be placed in a decorated sarcophagus, now ready to face eternity.

Mummies have always been a source of great mystery and fascination. The tales of mummy curses were wildly popular in their time, and people still flock to horror movies involving vengeful mummies. Museum displays, especially King Tut or Ramses II, remain a sure-fire draw, allowing patrons the chance for a remarkably preserved glimpse of ancient Egypt.

At first, mummification was so costly it remained the exclusive domain of the wealthy, usually royalty. However, when the middle class began adopting the procedure, the mummy population exploded. Soon people were mummifying everything—even crocodiles. The practice of mummifying the family cat was also common; the owners saw it as an offering to the cat goddess Bast.

Even those who could not afford to properly mummify their loved ones unknowingly contributed to the growing number of mummies. These folks buried their deceased in the Egyptian desert, where the hot, arid conditions dried out the bodies, creating natural mummies. When you consider that this burial art was in use for more than 3,000 years, it's not surprising that over time the bodies began piling up—literally.

So, with millions of mummies lying around, local entrepreneurs began looking for ways to cash in on these buried treasures. To them, mummies were a natural resource, not unlike oil, which could be extracted from the ground and sold at a heavy profit to eager buyers around the world.

Mummy Medicine

In medieval times, Egyptians began touting mummies for their secret medicinal qualities. European doctors began importing mummies, boiling off their oils and prescribing it to patients. The oil was used to treat a variety of disorders, including sore throats, coughs, epilepsy, poisoning, and skin disorders. Contemporary apothecaries also got into the act, marketing pulverized mummies to noblemen as a cure for nausea.

The medical establishment wasn't completely sold on the beneficial aspects of mummy medicine, however. Several doctors voiced their opinions against the practice, one writing that: "It ought to be rejected as loathsome and offensive," and another claiming: "This wicked kind of drugge doth nothing to help the diseased." A cholera epidemic, which broke out in Europe, was blamed on mummy bandages, and the use of mummy medicine was soon abandoned.

Mummy Merchants

Grave robbers, a common feature of 19th-century Egypt, made a huge profit from mummies. Arab traders would raid ancient tombs, sometimes making off with hundreds of bodies. These would be sold to visiting English merchants who, on returning to England, could resell them to wealthy buyers. Victorian socialites would buy mummies and hold fashionable parties, inviting friends over to view the unwrapping of their Egyptian prize.

Mummies in Museums

By the mid-19th century, museums were becoming common in Europe, and mummies were prized exhibits. Curators, hoping to make a name for their museums, would travel to Egypt and purchase a mummy to display back home. This provided a steady stream of revenue for the unscrupulous mummy merchants. In the 1850s, the Egyptian government finally stopped the looting of their priceless heritage. Laws were passed allowing only certified archaeologists access to mummy tombs, effectively putting the grave robbers out of business.

Mummy Myths

There are so many stories regarding the uses of mummies that it's often hard to separate fact from fiction. Some historians suggest the linens that comprised mummy wrappings were used by 19th-century American and Canadian industrialists to manufacture paper. At the time, there was a huge demand for paper, and suppliers often ran short of cotton rags—a key ingredient in the paper-making process. Although there's no concrete proof, some historians claim that when paper manufacturers ran out of rags, they imported mummies to use in their place.

Another curious claim comes courtesy of Mark Twain. In his popular 1869 travelogue *The Innocents Abroad*, Twain wrote: "The fuel [Egyptian train operators] use for the locomotive is composed of mummies three thousand years old, purchased by the ton or by the graveyard for that purpose." This item, almost assuredly meant as satire, was taken as fact by readers. However, there is no historical record of Egyptian trains running on burnt mummies. Besides, the mischievous Twain was never one to let a few facts get in the way of a good story. Perhaps those who believe the humorist's outlandish claim might offset it with another of his famous quotes: "A lie can travel halfway around the world while the truth is putting on its shoes."

A Brief History of Underwear

From fig leaves to bloomers to thongs, people have covered themselves a little or a lot, depending on social preferences and mores. Here is a brief history of the undergarment.

* The earliest and most simple undergarment was the loincloth—a long strip of material passed between the legs and around the waist. King Tutankhamen was buried with 145 of them, but the style didn't go out with the Egyptians. Loincloths are still worn in many Asian and African cultures.

* Medieval women wore a close-fitting undergarment called a chemise, and corsets began to appear in the 18th century. Early versions of the corset were designed to flatten a woman's bustline, but by the late 1800s, corsets were reconstructed to give women an exaggerated hourglass shape.

* Bras were invented in 1913 when American socialite Mary Phelps-Jacob tied two handkerchiefs together with ribbon. She patented the idea a year later. Maidenform introduced modern cup sizes in 1928.

* Around 1920, as women became more involved in sports such as tennis and bicycling, loose, comfortable bloomers replaced corsets as the undergarment of choice. The constricting corset soon fell out of favor altogether.

* The thong made its first public U.S. appearance at the 1939 World's Fair, when New York Mayor Fiorello LaGuardia required nude dancers to cover themselves, if only barely. Thongs gained popularity as swimwear in Brazil in the 1970s and are now a fashionable form of underwear in many parts of the world.

Poisoned Puddings and Puritanism: Harvard's Early Days

Today, Harvard is famed for a vast endowment, but its early days were marked by a struggle to get by with quarter-bushels of wheat donated by local farmers.

In 1640, the tiny college of Harvard was in crisis. Founded four years before by the Massachusetts Bay Colony, Harvard had a student body of nine; a "yard" liberated from cows; and a single, hated instructor. Harvard's 30-year-old schoolmaster, Nathaniel Eaton, was known to beat wayward students. Other students charged Eaton's wife, Elizabeth, of putting goat dung into their cornmeal porridge, or "hasty pudding." (Harvard's theatrical society is named for the dish.) Finally, Master Eaton went too far and was hauled into court after clubbing a scholar with a walnut-tree cudgel. He was also accused of embezzling 100 pounds (then an ample sum).

In 1639, Eaton and his wife were sent packing. Master Eaton returned to England, was made a vicar, then died in debtor's prison. Following the Eaton affair, Harvard's reputation lay in tatters; its operations were suspended, and its students were scattered.

The Roots of Learning

The money and work Massachusetts had put into the school seemed for naught. The colony's General Court had allotted 400 pounds for a college in what became known as Cambridge, Massachusetts—across the Charles River from Boston. The school was named for John Harvard, a clergyman from England's Cambridge University, which at the time was known to be a hotbed of Puritanism, the severe, idealistic faith opposed to the dominant Church of England.

John Harvard was a scholar whose family had known William Shakespeare. When the plague felled his brothers and his father, John inherited a considerable estate, including the Queen's Head Tavern. After immigrating to the Boston region, he became a preacher in Charleston, but his career was short. In 1638, at the age of 31, he died of consumption, having bequeathed money and his personal library to the planned college.

Comeback Under the First President

In 1640, the colony's founders were desperate for educational cachet. They offered the post of Harvard president to Henry Dunster, a new arrival from England and another graduate of Cambridge University.

The energetic Dunster tapped into the colony's inherent educational edge. Many of the new Puritan arrivals had studied at the Oxford and Cambridge academies: Some 130 alumni of the two schools were in New England by 1646. Dunster himself was a leading scholar in "Oriental" languages, that is, biblical tongues such as Hebrew.

Led primarily by a Protestant culture that stressed reading the Bible, Boston set up the first free grammar school in 1635; within 12 years, every town in Massachusetts was required by law to have one. Harvard's new president mandated a four-year graduation requirement and rode out angry students who protested over a commencement fee.

Dunster obtained Harvard's charter and authored the school's "Rules and Precepts." He bankrolled the facilities through donations of livestock and, over the course of 13 years, some 250 pounds of wheat. He took a modest salary, being underpaid through 14 years of service, and piled up personal debts. Fortunately, his wife, Elizabeth Glover, kept a printing press in their home. It was the American colonies' first press, and its profits underwrote her husband's work. Dunster managed to turn the school around. Harvard's reputation soared, and students from throughout the colonies, the Caribbean, and the mother country flocked to newly built dorms.

Religious Schisms and a President's Heresies

Yet Dunster tripped up on one of the many religious disputes roiling the Puritan colony. In 1648, it was a criminal offense to engage in "Blasphemy, Heresie, open contempt of the Word preached, Profanation of the Lord's Day"; separation of church and state was unknown.

A source of controversy was infant baptism, which the Puritan fathers required by law. Drawing on his biblical knowledge, Dunster noted that John the Baptist had baptized the adult Jesus, but he could find no biblical examples of children being baptized. In 1653, he refused to have his son Jonathan baptized. At Cambridge's Congregational Church, Dunster preached against "corruptions stealing into the Church, which every faithful Christian ought to [bear] witness against."

This put the Puritans of Boston and Cambridge in a quandary. Dunster's views made him a heretic, yet he was much liked for his work at the college. Early the next year, the colony's officers wrote that Dunster "hath by his practice and opinions rendered himself offensive to this government." They assembled a conference of 11 ministers and elders to interrogate him. Egged on by this assembly, in May 1654 the General Court forbade schools to employ those "that have manifested themselves unsound in the faith, or scandalous in their lives." Dunster resigned from Harvard.

The ex-president then petitioned the court to let him to stay in the colony until he could repay the many debts he'd accumulated from his work. Court authorities coldly responded that "they did not know of [such] extraordinary labor or sacrifices. For the space of 14 years we know of none." Dunster, with Elizabeth and their youngest child ill, then beseeched the court to at least let his family stay the winter. The magistrates agreed grudgingly, but the following spring they banished the Dunster family to the backwater town of Scituate. Harvard's first president died there four years later, at the age of 47.

Ludwig II: King of Castles

His desire to build fantasy castles and his patronage of, and infatuation with, famed composer Richard Wagner led many to refer to Bavarian King Ludwig II as the Dream King, the Swan King, the Fairytale King—even the Mad King.

Some say an insular childhood shaped Ludwig II into the eccentric he became. Peculiarities surrounded him from the moment he was born—his own birth announcement was delayed so the date could be moved one day forward to coincide with his grandfather's birthdate.

Ludwig was crowned king at age 18. That same year, Ludwig held his first meeting with composer Richard Wagner. His infatuation with Wagner eventually led Ludwig to pay the composer a stipend and fund construction of a theatre where Wagner's operas were performed.

After Bavaria's absorption into the new German Empire, Ludwig retreated into seclusion. From his mountain retreat in the Bavarian Alps, the king launched several grand construction projects that became the trademark of his reign.

Fantasies in Stone

One of Ludwig's most bizarre building projects included an underground lake—complete with electrical lights—at Linderhof Castle. Ludwig often rowed about the lake in a shell-shape boat while shore-side singers performed operas. The castle's architecture was influenced by French King Louis XIV and was the king's only castle project to be completed.

The most famous of Ludwig's castles is New Castle Hohenschwangau. Several swan motifs were incorporated into the castle's design, leading the edifice to be renamed Neuschwanstein, or "New Swan Stone," after his death. Built high above Pollat Gorge, Neuschwanstein is a mix of Byzantine and Gothic design elements that rate it as one of the most recognized castles in the world. In fact, Disney used it as inspiration when designing the Sleeping Beauty castle featured at Disneyland.

Despite a 22-year construction period, only 14 rooms of Neuschwanstein were ever completed. The castle's interior features several wall paintings, which depict scenes from Wagner's operas. Never one to forgo the modern trappings of life, Ludwig built this castle with several state-of-the-art features, including a forced-air heating system and a flush toilet.

Ludwig's third castle, Herrenchiemsee, was located on an island in Lake Chiemsee. It was modeled after the central section of the Palace of Versailles and contained a reproduction of the palace's ambassador's staircase. Unfortunately, Ludwig died during its construction, and Herrenchiemsee was never completed.

A World of Dreams

On June 8, 1886, Ludwig was declared "mentally disordered" by a psychiatrist who hadn't even examined him. On June 10, the king was declared insane and was deposed by his uncle. Two days later, Ludwig was arrested and taken to Castle Berg, south of Munich. After taking a walk along Lake Starnberg with the doctor who had declared him unfit to rule, Ludwig was discovered floating in the shallow water. The doctor's body was found in the water as well. The king's death was ruled a suicide despite the fact that autopsy results showed no water in Ludwig's lungs. This finding has led some to speculate that the king was murdered. On June 19, Ludwig's remains were interred in the crypt of Saint Michael's. In accordance with tradition, his heart was placed in a silver urn and interred in the Chapel of the Miraculous Image.

African Exploration Becomes Europe's Heart of Darkness

The improbable meeting of Dr. David Livingston and Henry Morton Stanley in 1871 was perhaps the greatest celebrity interview of all time, a high point in African exploration that would leave as its legacy one of the most brutal colonial empires in history.

It had been five years since Scottish missionary David Livingston disappeared into central Africa to find the source of the Nile, and he was presumed dead by his sponsor, Britain's Royal Geographical Society. New York newspaper magnate James Gordon Bennett, Jr., saw the potential for a great story in Livingston's disappearance. He dispatched young war correspondent Henry Morton Stanley to find him.

Dr. Livingston, I Presume?

Stanley led a large party of guards and porters into uncharted territory in March 1871. Within a few days, his stallion was dead from tsetse flies, and dozens of his carriers were deserting with valuable supplies. Over the months that followed, his party was decimated by tropical disease. They endured encounters with hostile tribes—and at one point were pursued by cannibals chanting, "Meat! Meat!" Finally, on November 10, 1871, Stanley found the ailing Livingston at a settlement on Lake Tanganyika in present-day Tanzania, supposedly greeting him with "Dr. Livingston, I presume?"

Though most of his party had perished and he had won only a handful of converts to Christianity, Livingston had become the first European to see Victoria Falls. Stanley's dispatches to the *New York Herald*, which told the world of Livingston's discoveries as well as Stanley's own adventures, were the media sensation of the age.

Fame and Misfortune

Upon his return to Great Britain, Stanley was met with public ridicule by scientists and the press, who doubted his claim that he found Livingston and questioned the veracity of his other accounts as well. Though his book, *How I Found Livingston*, was a best seller, Stanley was deeply wounded by his detractors.

Indeed, Stanley was an unlikely hero. Born John Rowland, he was a bastard child whose mother gave him up to a workhouse. He left Britain at the age of 17 to work as a deckhand on a merchant vessel. However, he jumped ship in New Orleans and took the name of an English planter, who he claimed had adopted him. Contemporary historians doubt that Stanley ever met the man.

Stanley's adult life was an improbable series of adventures and lies. He served, unremarkably, on both sides during the Civil War and worked unsuccessfully at a variety of trades before trying his hand at journalism. He reported on the Indian wars in the West and the Colorado gold rush. Stanley came to the attention of newspaper magnate Bennett while reporting for the *New York Herald* on a British military expedition into Abyssinia. His colorful writing style won him the assignment to find Livingston.

The Greatest African Explorer

Stanley may have found in Livingston the father figure he never had. His accounts of the missionary created a portrait of a saintly doctor who, inspired by his opposition to Africa's brutal slave trade, had opened the continent to Western civilization and Christianity. When Livingston died in 1873, Stanley served as a pallbearer at his funeral in Westminster Abbey. A year later, he set out on another epic expedition to complete Livingston's work. Over the next three years, Stanley established Lake Victoria as the source of the Nile and led his party down the uncharted Congo River—a 2,900-mile course that transversed the continent.

Though acclaimed as the greatest of African explorers, Stanley's accounts of his brutal methods—such as whipping African porters and gunning down tribespeople with modern weaponry—brought public outrage in Britain. After examining his original notes and letters, however, some contemporary historians believe that he often exaggerated his exploits, including the numbers of Africans supposedly killed, to elevate his own legend.

"The Horror!"

Unable to persuade the British government to employ him, Stanley undertook a third journey in 1879 under the sponsorship of Belgium's King Leopold II. He

established 22 trading posts along the Congo River, laying the foundation for a vast colonial empire that would exploit the rubber and ivory trades at the expense of millions of African lives. Stanley earned the African nickname Bula Matari, or "breaker of rocks," on account of his ruthless determination to build roads linking the Congo's waterways. Natives were beaten, tortured, and killed under his command. This third expedition led to the scramble for Africa among European nations, culminating in the Berlin Conference of 1885, which divided the continent among colonial powers. Leopold II established his rights to the so-called Congo Free State, his private enterprise encompassing most of the Congo Basin. Historians estimate that as many as 13 million Congolese were murdered or died from disease or overwork under Leopold's regime, inspiring Joseph Conrad's novel *Heart of Darkness.*

A last African expedition between 1887 and 1889 further tarnished Stanley's name. Sent to rescue a dubious ally in southern Sudan, he left behind a rear column whose leaders—former British army officers and aristocrats—fell into sadism. Though most of his party perished and much more African blood was shed, Stanley helped establish British territorial claims in East Africa and opened a path to further colonization. Finally marrying and adopting the bastard grandchild of a Welsh nun, Stanley retired from exploration to write books and conduct lecture tours. He won a seat in Parliament in 1895 and was knighted by Queen Victoria in 1899. He died in 1904 at the age of 63. Although he was considered a national hero, he was denied burial next to Livingston at Westminster Abbey due to his mixed reputation.

Blooming Bust in the Dutch Republic

Can a mere flower incite great nationalist passion? Well, if it's a tulip, it can. What might be dubbed "Tulipmania" swept what is now Holland in 1636 and 1637. The flowers' popularity turned the pretty plants into serious money spinners and encouraged a competitive fad among the nouveau riche. Suddenly, the tulip was a coveted status symbol.

The instigator of all this was a French-born botanist named Carolus Clusius, who lived and died before the craze hit. Born in 1526 and originally educated as a lawyer, Clusius was encouraged by a professor to switch his studies to botany. He subsequently traveled the world gathering plant specimens and became one of Europe's leading botanists. His reputation was so sterling that Austrian Emperor Maximilian II appointed him court physician and overseer of the royal medicinal garden.

In 1593, Clusius settled in the Netherlands, where he was appointed prefect for the newly established horticulture academy at the University of Leiden. That fall, Clusius planted a teaching garden and a private plot that showcased hundreds of varieties of plants, including several hundred tulip bulbs given to him by his friend, Ogier Ghiselin de Busbecq, Austrian Ambassador to the Ottoman Empire.

Prior to Clusius, no Dutch person had ever seen a tulip bulb or blossom. The rarity and beauty of the new flower caused a national sensation. Members of the aristocracy clamored to add tulips to their private gardens. When Clusius declined to sell any of his private stock, many were stolen from his garden. One nighttime raid netted thieves more than 100 bulbs.

Big Money in the Dutch Republic

Carolus Clusius died in 1609, but the engine he had set in motion continued to chug without him. In the 1620s, the Dutch Republic began its ascent to global power, gaining a trade monopoly with the East Indies and Japan. Sound government monetary policy demanded that national currency be backed 10 percent by gold and silver deposits, held by the Bank of Amsterdam. The republic was flush with cash.

Money supply in the Dutch Republic was increased further by an influx of precious metals, which were traded for paper currency, as well as by the Dutch East India Company's seizure of Portuguese ships laden with gold, silver, and jewels. At the height of Tulipmania, the Bank of Amsterdam's deposits increased by more than 40 percent. People had more money to spend than ever before, and they became bold in an atmosphere that was ripe for speculation.

My Kingdom for a Tulip

The tulip quickly became a status symbol. Members of the upper class spent huge amounts of money to acquire rare bulbs. Some sums were utterly ridiculous. Consider that during the 1600s, the average Dutch worker earned 150 florins per year. In 1623, one particularly rare tulip bulb sold for 1,000 florins. In another famous sale, an extraordinary Semper Augustsus bulb sold for 6,000 florins. The price per pound of some bulbs reached the equivalent price of a modest house.

By 1636, a structured, but unregulated, futures market had developed for the tulip trade. Most of the trading occurred in local taverns, where bulbs were bought and resold many times before actual delivery. The Dutch referred to this practice as *windhandel,* or wind trade, because payment for the bulbs occurred only when they were dug from the ground in the summer, after the plant had bloomed and died back. Local-government legislation designed to curtail speculation did little to affect the trade.

The Flower Economy Crashes

In February 1637, the Dutch guild of florists, which had been marginalized by the wildcat trading, decreed that all futures contracts were now mere options contracts. With a futures contract, both parties must fulfill the contract's terms. With an options contract, the holder has the right, but is not obligated, to exercise the contract. The florist guild's decision allowed buyers to break their contracts for a fraction of actual value. On April 27,

1637, the Dutch government canceled all tulip contracts with a decree stating that tulips were a product, not an investment. Between this and an oversupply of bulbs, the value of tulips plummeted and the market crashed. Buyers refused to honor their contracts and simply walked away from their deals. Growers were not only unable to sell their stock, they suddenly had no hope of collecting any of the money owed to them. Between 1635 and 1637, the number of bankruptcies in Amsterdam doubled. Prices for bulbs stabilized at reasonable levels shortly after the collapse, but many Dutch were so discouraged they never entered the tulip market again.

Love Affair Continues

Today, almost 400 years after the crash, the Dutch love affair with tulips is still going strong. Holland's flower bulb farms currently produce about three billion bulbs every year, with approximately two billion of those exported to other countries.

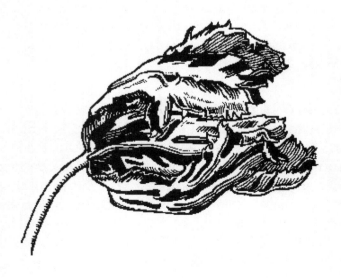

Pulling the Wool over the Eyes of NYC

Throughout the 1860s and 1870s, a man named William "Boss" Tweed controlled New York City politics—and, subsequently, New York City itself. Graft, payoffs, cheating, and a healthy dose of high-quality corruption were the order of the day.

It All Started with Tammany Hall

As the United States struggled to stand on its own following the American Revolution, political organizations began to spring up across the East Coast. The biggest and most influential was the Tammany, named after Native American Chief Tamanend. Founded on May 12, 1789, it was first a social and political organization. Then, under the leadership of Aaron Burr, the group embraced the politics of Thomas Jefferson and began supporting candidates. It was no small coincidence that Burr was elected vice president in 1800.

The strength of Tammany continued to grow, aiding the presidential election of Andrew Jackson in 1828 and 1832. By then, the powerful Democratic faction literally ran all of the politics in New York City, based out of their huge headquarters called "Tammany Hall." The organization became known by the same name.

Tammany Hall soon became a tool of the Irish Catholic community, which had quickly formed in New York City after the potato famine in Ireland drove its inhabitants to the shores of Manhattan in the mid-1840s. By the mid-1850s, Tammany Hall controlled the outcome of mayoral races, as well as other elected offices. Skilled in the art of politics, the leaders of this political machine kept New York City running—and their pockets filled.

Who's the Boss?

In New York City, a young Scottish-Irish bookkeeper and volunteer firefighter named William Tweed used his municipal position and connections to become elected as an alderman in New York City in 1851. He soon became a member of Congress and, in 1857, became the leader of Tammany Hall.

The next 14 years became a swirl of voting fraud, judge-buying, and contract kickbacks for "Boss" Tweed and his cronies. In one instance, a carpenter received more than $360,000 for work done in a building that had very little wood in it. A furniture dealer was paid nearly $180,000 for three conference tables and 40 chairs. A plasterer received more than $130,000 for a mere two days of work. Tweed orchestrated the construction of the New York County Courthouse—a task that took nearly 20 years (2 years past his death, in fact) and cost $13 million. It was estimated that the project's price tag should have been half that figure. When an investigation was conducted into the excessive amount, the resulting report cost nearly $8,000 to print. The owner of the printing company was William Tweed.

Getting Tweed Off

The "Tweed Ring," which included the mayor and city comptroller, profited to the tune of an estimated $100 million to $200 million by the time their activities were exposed in 1871. New York newspapers and magazines, featuring unflattering political cartoons of Tweed by illustrator Thomas Nast, revealed the graft under the Tweed Ring, and the "Boss" was brought to trial in 1874. Found guilty of embezzlement, he was sentenced to 12 years in prison, but served only a year on appeal.

Arrested the next year on a separate charge, Tweed escaped to Cuba but was found and held by Cuban officials. Before U.S. marshals could claim Tweed, however, he bolted to Spain. The Spanish government immediately grabbed him as he landed. William Tweed was returned to a New York City jail (a jail that he may very well have had built under his regime), where he died two years later in April 1878. He was only 55.

Terrible Ivan

Ivan the Terrible had an unhealthy dose of paranoia. It must have been his upbringing. As a child prince in Moscow, Ivan was under the thumb of boyars, or Russia's nobles. Feuding noble families such as the Shuiskis would break into young Ivan's palace, robbing, murdering, and even skinning alive one of the boy's advisors. The orphan (his mother had been poisoned) took out his frustrations on animals, poking out their eyes or tossing them off the palace roof. In 1543, at age 13, Ivan took some personal revenge, and had Andrei Shuiski thrown to the dogs—literally. After other vile acts, he'd sometimes publicly repent—by banging his head violently on the ground.

When his beloved wife Anastasia died in 1560 (Ivan beat his head on her coffin), the boyars refused allegiance to his young son Dmitri. Then Ivan really became terrifying. He set up the Oprichniki, a group of hand-picked thugs. After his forces sacked the city of Novgorod in 1570, he had its "archbishop sewn up in a bearskin and then hunted to death by a pack of hounds." Women and children fared no better; they were tied to sleds and sent into the freezing Volkhov River.

Over time, Ivan had the lover of his fourth wife impaled and had his seventh wife drowned. Perhaps afflicted by encephalitis, and likely by syphilis, his behavior grew ever stranger. He beat up his son's wife, who then miscarried, and later beat his son Ivan to death with a royal scepter (then beat his head on the coffin).

Ivan the Terrible may well have been mad as a hatter, and by the same cause that drove 19th-century hatmakers insane—mercury poisoning. When his body was exhumed in the 1960s, his bones were found to have toxic levels of the metal.

The Legendary Mohawk Ironworkers

Employing the fearless Mohawk Indians as ironworkers, the Dominion Bridge Company set a constructive force into motion that six generations later has—in no small part—built up the entire New York City skyline.

In 1886, Dominion crews were building a cantilevered bridge for the Canadian Pacific railway to cross the St. Lawrence river, near Montreal. The construction path skirted an island reservation of the Mohawk nation Kahnawake, and, to ease any qualms that the bridge's new neighbors might raise, Dominion agreed to hire day-laborers from the reservation.

Spanning New Heights

A Dominion official, consulting internal company documents and memoranda, told *The New Yorker* in 1949 that the Mohawks hired for the job were given menial tasks like unloading materials for the actual steelworkers to use. However, the official noted, "They were dissatisfied with this arrangement and would come out on the bridge itself every chance they got. It was quite impossible to keep them off. As the work progressed, it became apparent to all concerned that these Indians were very odd in that they did not have any fear of heights. If not watched, they would climb up into the spans and walk around up there as cool and collected as the toughest of our riveters, most of whom at that period were old sailing ship men especially picked for the experience in working aloft."

And so a legend was born. Sprouting cities across the American and Canadian northeast had no shortage of jobs for skywalkers who could wield a rivet gun. Kahnawake residents soon found work as actual riveters at the Soo Bridge, spanning Sault Ste. Marie, Ontario, and Michigan—a job that served as vocational college for these previously unskilled tradespeople. By 1907, Kahnawake was home to some 70 bridgemen, who would hop as an ensemble from one project to the next.

Disaster Strikes

But 1907 was also when disaster transformed this would-be trade union. Hailed as one of the early 20th century's great engineering marvels, the Québec Bridge spanned the St. Lawrence from Québec City to Levis, Québec. On August 29, minutes after a foreman ended the workday with the sound of his whistle, the Québec Bridge collapsed, sending 76 men to a watery grave. In Kahnawake, which lost 33 bridgemen, this tragedy is known to this day simply as "The Disaster."

New York, New York

After The Disaster, the village women gathered in this matriarchal society and decided that to avoid another widespread tragedy, their ironworking husbands, fathers, and brothers would never again work en masse as a Nation. The practical upshot of this policy decision was to scatter Mohawk ironworkers to the winds, which led many of them to New York at a moment in history when buildings were pushing up like rows of sunflowers. From the 1920s onward, Mohawks from Kahnawake (and Akwesasne, near Québec City) riveted their way across patches of sky that became the Empire State Building, the Chrysler Building, Rockefeller Center, The Triborough Bridge, and of course, the World Trade Center.

On the morning of September 11, 2001, skywalkers from Kahnawake raced down to New York to be some of the first construction crews to dismantle what uncles, fathers, and cousins had assembled three decades ago.

Today, Mohawks from Kahnawake and Akwesasne are members of ironworkers' union locals in Montreal and New York, as well as New Jersey, Boston, Detroit, and Kentucky.

Order in the Court?
Animals on Trial

The year was 1386. In the French city of Falaise, a child was killed and partially devoured by a sow and her six piglets. Locals refused to let such a heinous crime go unpunished. However, rather than killing the sow, they brought her to trial. The pig was dressed in men's clothing, tried for murder, convicted, and hanged from the gallows in the public square.

Porkers weren't the only animals to face trial during medieval times. Bees, snakes, horses, and bulls were also charged with murder. Foxes were charged with theft. Rats were charged with damaging barley. In the early 1700s, Franciscan friars in Brazil brought "white ants" (probably termites) to trial because "the said ants did feloniously burrow beneath the foundation of the monastery and undermine the cellars . . . threatening its total ruin."

History

The first record of animal trials comes from Athens. More than 2,000 years ago, the Athenians instituted a special court to try murderous objects (such as stones and beams) as well as animals that caused human deaths. They believed that in order to protect moral equilibrium and to prevent the wrath of the Furies, these murders had to be avenged.

Animal trials peaked in the Middle Ages, ranging from the 9th century to as late as the 18th century. During this time, people believed that animals committed crimes against humans and that, like humans, animals were morally and legally responsible for their actions. As a result, animals received the same punishment as humans, ranging from a knock on the head to excommunication or death.

Legal Rights

Animals accused of crimes during Europe's Middle Ages received much the same rights under the law as humans, which included a fair trial. Domestic animals were often tried in civil courts and punished individually. Animals that existed in groups (such as weevils, eels, horseflies, locusts, caterpillars, and worms) were usually tried in ecclesiastical courts. They weren't stretched on the rack to extract confessions, nor were they hanged with individual nooses. Instead, they received a group malediction or anathema.

The accused animals were also entitled to legal representation. When the weevils in the French village of St. Julien were accused of threatening the vineyards in 1587, Pierre Rembaud argued in their defense. The innocent weevils should not be blamed, said Rembaud. Rather, the villagers should recognize God's wrath and don sackcloth. The court ruled in favor of the weevils and gave them their own parcel of land. As for the six little piglets in Falaise? They also must have had good counsel—they were acquitted on the grounds of their youth and their mother's poor example.

Capital Punishment

Murder wasn't the only crime to carry a death sentence. Often, animals accused of witchcraft or other heinous crimes received similar punishment. In 1474, a cock was burned at the stake in Basel, Switzerland, for the crime of laying an egg. As was widely understood, this could result in the birth of a basilisk, a monster that could wreak havoc in a person's home.

Pigs were often brought to the gallows for infanticide (a perennial problem since 900-pound sows often ran free). A mother pig smothering her infants was most likely an accident, but in those times people saw it as a sign of evil thanks to the Biblical account of the demon-possessed herd at Gadarenes.

Animals had slim hopes for survival when accused of severe crimes. However, there is the amazing account of a jenny that was saved when the parish priest and the citizens signed a certificate that proclaimed her innocence. It stated that they had known the "she-ass" for four years and that "she had always shown herself to be virtuous and well-behaved both at home and abroad and had never given occasion of scandal to anyone."

Contemporary Courtrooms

Although animals are not tried as humans in the United States, they are not immune to the gavel. In April 2007, a 300-pound donkey named Buddy entered the court-room at the North Dallas Government Center in Texas.

While technically it was Buddy's owner who was on trial, the donkey was accused of the "crime." His owner's neighbor had been complaining about Buddy's braying and foul odor.

When the defense attorney asked Buddy if he was the said donkey, Buddy twitched his ears and remained silent. For the next few minutes, he was calm and po-lite—hardly the obnoxious beast that had been described in the accusations.

While the jury pondered, the neighbors reached an agreement. The day ended peacefully. Buddy—like his ancestors—had his day in court.

Philo T. Farnsworth: The Teenager Who Invented Television

Philo T. Farnsworth's brilliance was obvious from an early age. In 1919, when he was only 12, he amazed his parents and older siblings by fixing a balky electrical generator on their Idaho farm. By age 14, he had built an electrical laboratory in the family attic and was setting his alarm for 4 a.m. so he could get up and read science journals for an hour before doing chores.

Farnsworth hated the drudgery of farming. He often daydreamed solutions to scientific problems as he worked. During the summer of 1921, he was particularly preoccupied with the possibility of transmitting moving pictures through the air.

Around the same time, big corporations like RCA were spending millions of research dollars trying to find a practical way to do just that. As it turned out, most of their work was focused on a theoretical dead-end. Back in 1884, German scientist Paul Nipkow had patented a device called the Nipkow disc. By rotating the disc rapidly while passing light through tiny holes, an illusion of movement could be created. In essence, the Nipkow disc was a primitive way to scan images. Farnsworth doubted that this mechanical method of scanning could ever work fast enough to send images worth watching. He was determined to find a better way.

His "Eureka!" moment came as he cultivated a field with a team of horses. Swinging the horses around to do another row, Farnsworth glanced back at the furrows behind him. Suddenly, he realized that scanning could be done electronically, line-by-line. Light could be converted into streams of electrons and then back again with such rapidity that the eye would be fooled. He immediately set about designing what would one day be called the cathode ray tube. Seven years would pass, however, before he was able to display a working model of his mental breakthrough.

Upon graduating from high school, Farnsworth enrolled at the University of Utah but dropped out after a year because he could no longer afford the tuition. Almost immediately, though, he found financial backers and moved to San Francisco to continue his research. The cathode ray tube he developed there became the basis for all television. In 1930, a researcher from RCA named Vladimir Zworykin visited Farnsworth's California laboratory and copied his invention. When Farnsworth refused to sell his patent to RCA for $100,000, the company sued him. The legal wrangling continued for many years and, though Farnsworth eventually earned royalties from his invention, he never did get wealthy from it.

By the time Farnsworth died in 1971, there were more homes on Earth with televisions than with indoor plumbing. Ironically, the man most responsible for television appeared on the small screen only once. It was a 1957 appearance on the game show *I've Got a Secret*. Farnsworth's secret was that "I invented electric television at the age of 15." When none of the panelists guessed Farnsworth's secret, he left the studio with his winnings—$80 and a carton of Winston cigarettes.

Shroud of Turin: Real or Fake?

Measuring roughly 14 feet long by 3 feet wide, the Shroud of Turin features the front and back image of a man who was 5 feet, 9 inches tall. The man was bearded and had shoulder-length hair parted down the middle. Dark stains on the Shroud are consistent with blood from a crucifixion.

First publicly displayed in 1357, the Shroud of Turin has apparent ties to the Knights of Templar. At the time of its first showing, the Shroud was in the hands of the family of Geoffrey de Charney, a Templar who had been burned at the stake in 1314 along with Jacques de Molay. Some accounts say it was the Knights who removed the cloth from Constantinople, where it was kept in the 13th century.

Some believe the Shroud of Turin is the cloth that Jesus was wrapped in after his death. All four gospels mention that the body of Jesus was covered in a linen cloth prior to the resurrection.

Others assert that the cloth shrouded Jacques de Molay after he was tortured by being nailed to a door.

Still others contend that the Shroud was evidence of early photographic experiments of Leonardo da Vinci. He mentioned working with "optics" in some of his diaries and wrote his notes in a sort of mirrored hand-writing style, some say, to keep his experiments secret from the church.

Is the Shroud of Turin authentic? In 1988, scientists using carbon-dating concluded that the material in the Shroud was from between AD 1260 to 1390, which seems to exclude the possibility that the Shroud bears the image of Jesus.

Crossdressers Throughout History

Clothes, the saying goes, make the man. For some men, clothes also make the woman. And vice versa.

A transvestite wears garments of the opposite sex and sometimes assumes alternate cross-gender identity as part of daily life. Women dress as men; men dress as women. For the record, transvestism, though less common than, say, Republicanism, is not a mental illness or a perversion. And transvestites are not usually transsexuals (men and women who undergo hormonal and/or surgical sex change); in fact, the typical transvestite is heterosexual and comfortable with his/her gender.

Transvestite activity traces back to the earliest days of recorded civilization and recurs throughout the span of human history, across all societies and walks of life. Although ordinarily a private inclination, transvestism has occasionally been very public.

She's in Charge Here

More than 3,400 years ago, a woman named Hatshepsut ruled Egypt as a king. Her story is the first recorded
instance of transvestism in history. Hatshepsut, part of
the 18th royal dynasty of ancient Egypt, became pha-
raoh when her husband, Thutmose II, died and the heir
to the throne was only nine years old. So Hatshepsut
initially ruled as regent, in her capacity as both aunt and
stepmother to the true royal heir. But sometime between
the second and seventh years of her reign (1477–72 BC),
Hatshepsut assumed the trappings of manhood and king-
hood. She was often depicted wearing a false beard and
without apparent breasts. She commanded that she be
addressed as "he" and changed her name to the masculine Hatshepsu.

Like Hatshepsut, many female-to-male crossdressers
throughout history have donned male garb for the social,
political, and even military opportunities they would
never have had access to in the traditional roles of their
gender. For instance, James Barry (1795–1865), a surgeon in the British Army, was a woman working as a
man and was unsuspected for years. It was only at Barry's
death that the attending physicians were astounded to
discover that their comrade was a woman—or, according to some reports, a hermaphrodite (a person born
with the complete or partial genitals of both sexes). Less
open to dispute are the lives of stagecoach driver Charlie
Parkhurst (d. 1879) and New York political figure Mur-
ray Hall (1831–1901)—both of whom lived their entire
adult lives as men, only to be discovered at their deaths
to have been women. And the female jazz musician Billy
Tipton (1914–1989) pursued a life and career during
which everyone, including her wife, thought her to be
a man.

Royal Surprises

One of history's most popular examples of a woman in men's plumage came in 1429, when the 17-year-old peasant Joan of Arc bravely presented herself to the court of French heir apparent Prince Charles as God's appointed ruler of the force that was destined to over-throw occupying English forces. Her male attire, too, she said, was God's will. When Charles handed Joan command of the peasant army with which she would make history, the prince overlooked the capital crime that the Grand Inquisition, two years later, would not: "Condemn[ing herself] in being unwilling to wear the customary clothing of [the female] sex."

The French court also offers up a royal story of transves-tism oriented in the other direction: King Henri III, who ruled from 1574–1589, was infamous for wearing gowns, makeup, earrings, and perfume. He sometimes com-manded that he be referred to as "Her Majesty," and he kept a court of "mignons"—young male favorites whom the king dressed as ladies of the night.

The history of male-to-female crossdressing cuts through all social castes and sexual persuasions. The story of Henri III, married and evidently bisexual, splits the difference between heterosexual transvestites (such as the contemporary British comedian Eddie Izzard and the famed American B-movie director of the 1950s Edward D. Wood, Jr.) and the campier standards of generally gay drag queens, such as pop star RuPaul.

Fun in the New World

Doomed to be outcasts according to American and European traditions, transvestites have held prominent roles in some non-Western cultures. Aboriginal nations across what is now North, Central, and South America treated crossdressing and cross-gender roleplaying as acceptable parts of society. "Strange country this," wrote one Caucasian, circa 1850, about the Crow nation of the Yellowstone River Valley in North America, "where males assume the dress and perform the duties of females, while women turn men and mate with their own sex!" Aboriginal women in what is today Brazil were often welcomed as male warriors and hunters—which in 1576 inspired the Portuguese explorer Pedro de Magalhaes to name the country's great river after the famous matriarchal society from Greek mythology, the Amazons.

A source of disquiet in some societies, and an invitation to prestige and respect in others, transvestism will be a part of human sexuality for as long as there are gender boundaries to be crossed and explored.

The Bloody Countess

In the early 1600s, villagers in the Carpathian region of Hungary whispered amongst themselves about a vampire living in the local castle. An investigation brought to light the brutal atrocities of Countess Elizabeth Bathory, who was accused of torturing hundreds of young girls to death and bathing in their blood.

The Best Sort of People

Elizabeth Bathory was the daughter of one of the oldest and most influential bloodlines in Hungary. Her wedding in 1575 to Ferenc Nadasdy was enough of an event to warrant written approval and an expensive gift from the Holy Roman Emperor himself. Of course, there were rumors that a streak of insanity ran in Elizabeth's family; some rumors hint that she may have been related to Vlad the Impaler. However, nobles of the time were given wide latitude when it came to eccentric behavior.

Ferenc would go on to become one of the greatest Hungarian military heroes of the age. He was a battle-hardened man, but even so, his own wife made him nervous. He was aware that she treated the servants even more harshly than he did—and he had no reservations when it came to punishing the help. He was known to place flaming oil-covered wicks between the toes of lazy servants. But Elizabeth's punishments far exceeded even this brutality. Ferenc saw evidence of this when he discovered a servant who had been covered with honey and tied to a tree to be ravaged by ants as punishment for stealing food. Still, Ferenc spent a great deal of time away at war, and someone had to manage his castle. Elizabeth took on the task willingly; in turn, he turned a deaf ear to complaints about her activities.

From Punishment to Atrocity

Initially, Elizabeth's punishments may have been no more harsh than those imposed by her contemporaries. However, with her husband's lengthy absences and eventual death, Elizabeth found that she had virtually no restrictions on her behavior. A series of lovers of both sexes occupied some of her time. She also dabbled in black magic, though this was not uncommon in an age when paganism and Christianity were contending for supremacy. She spent hours doing nothing more than gazing into a wraparound mirror of her own design, crafted to hold her upright so that she would not tire as she examined her own reflection. The exacting fashion of the day required Elizabeth, always a vain woman, to constantly worry over the angle of her collar or the style of her hair.

She had a small army of body servants constantly by her side to help maintain her appearance. They were often required to attend to their mistress in the nude as an expression of subservience. If they failed in their duties, Elizabeth would strike out, pummeling them into the ground. On one notable occasion, a servant pulled too hard when combing Elizabeth's hair; Elizabeth struck the offender in the face hard enough to cause the girl's blood to spray and cover the countess. Initially furious, Elizabeth discovered she liked the sensation, believing her skin was softer, smoother, and more translucent after the experience.

A Taste for Blood

The incident led to the legends, which cannot be confirmed, that Elizabeth Bathory took to bathing in the blood of virgins to maintain her youthful appearance. One rumor has her inviting 60 peasant girls for a banquet, only to lock them in a room and slaughter them one at a time, letting their blood run over her body. Though that incident may be apocryphal, it is certain that the countess began torturing girls without restraint. Aided by two trustworthy servants who recruited a never-ending supply of hopeful girls from the poor families of the area, she would beat her victims with a club until they were scarcely recognizable. When her arms grew tired, she had her two assistants continue the punishment as she watched. She had a spiked iron cage specially built and would place a girl within it, shaking the cage as the individual bounced from side to side and was impaled over and over on the spikes. She drove pins into lips and breasts, held flames to pubic regions, and once pulled a victim's mouth open so forcefully that the girl's cheeks split. Perhaps most chillingly, allegations of vampirism and cannibalism arose when Elizabeth began biting her victims, tearing off the flesh with her bare teeth. On one occasion, too sick to rise from her bed, the countess demanded that a peasant girl be brought to her. She roused herself long enough to bite chunks from the girl's face, shoulders, and nipples. Elizabeth's chambers had to be covered with fresh cinders daily to prevent the countess from slipping on the bloody floor.

Justice for the Countess

Eventually, even the cloak of nobility couldn't hide Elizabeth's atrocities. The situation was compounded by the fact that she got sloppy, killing in such numbers that the local clergy refused to perform any more burials. Thereafter, she would throw bodies to the wolves in full view of local villagers, who naturally complained to the authorities. The final straw was when Elizabeth began to prey on the minor aristocracy as well as the peasants; the disappearance of people of higher birth could not be tolerated. The king decided that something had to be done, and in January 1611, a trial was held. Elizabeth was not allowed to testify, but her assistants were compelled to—condemning themselves to death in the process—and they provided eyewitness accounts of the terrible practices of the countess. Especially damning was the discovery of a list, in Elizabeth's own handwriting, describing more than 600 people she had tortured to death.

Elizabeth Bathory was convicted of perpetrating "horrifying cruelties" and was sentenced to be walled up alive in her own castle. She survived for nearly four years but was finally discovered dead on August 21, 1614, by one of her guards who had risked a peek through a tiny food slot. The countess was unrepentant to the end.

A Gay Time in the Oval Office?

Before he became U.S. president, the unmarried James Buchanan enjoyed a long, close association with his housemate, William R. King—so close that unconfirmed speculation about the pair still swirls after more than 150 years. Was Buchanan—the nation's only bachelor chief executive—also its first homosexual president?

The year 1834 was a momentous one for 42-year-old James Buchanan. Already a veteran political leader and diplomat, Buchanan won a seat in the U.S. Senate and formed a friendship with the man who would be his dearest companion for the next two decades. Buchanan and his chum, William Rufus de Vane King, a U.S. senator from Alabama, became virtually inseparable. They shared quarters in Washington, D.C., for 15 years. Capitol wits referred to the partners—who attended social events together—as "the Siamese twins."

Buchanan's bond with Senator King was so close that the future president described it as a "communion." In praising his friend as "among the best, purest, and most consistent public men I have ever known," Buchanan added that King was a "very gay, elegant-looking fellow." The adjective "gay," however, didn't mean "homosexual" back then. It commonly meant "merry." It's also useful to understand that it was not unusual for educated men to wax rhapsodic about other men during the 19th century. Admiring rather than sexual, this sort of language signified shared values and deep respect.

Historians rightly point out a lack of evidence that either of the bachelors found men sexually attractive. They note that when Buchanan was younger, he asked a Pennsylvania heiress to marry him. (She broke off the engagement.) Later, he was known to flirt with fashionable women.

Buchanan's "Wife"

Whatever the nature of his relationship with Buchanan, King seemed to consider it something more than casual. After the Alabaman became U.S. minister to France in 1844, he wrote home from Paris, expressing his worry that Buchanan would "procure an associate who will cause you to feel no regret at our separation."

Buchanan did not find such a replacement, but it was apparently not for want of trying. He wrote to another friend of his attempts to ease the loneliness caused by King's absence: "I have gone a wooing to several gentlemen, but have not succeeded with any one of them . . . ."

Sometimes the pair drew derisive jibes from their peers. The jokes often targeted King, a bit of a dandy with a fondness for silk scarves. In a private letter, Tennessee Congressman Aaron V. Brown used the pronoun "she" to refer to the senator, and called him Buchanan's "wife." President Andrew Jackson mocked King as "Miss Nancy" and "Aunt Fancy."

High-Flying Careers Derailed

Despite the childish jokes, both Buchanan and King advanced to ever-more-important federal posts. President James K. Polk selected Buchanan as his secretary of state in 1845. King won the office of U.S. vice president (running on a ticket with Franklin Pierce) in 1852. Voters elected Buchanan to the White House four years later. Unfortunately, neither of the friends distinguished himself in the highest office he reached. King fell ill and died less than a month after taking the oath as vice president. Erupting conflicts over slavery and states' rights marred Buchanan's single term in the Oval Office. Historians give him failing marks for his lack of leadership as the Civil War loomed. The pro-slavery chief executive (he was a Pennsylvania Democrat) opposed secession of the Southern states but argued that the federal government had no authority to use force to stop it. As a result, Buchanan made no effort to save the Union, leaving that task to his successor, Abraham Lincoln.

What's Sex Got To Do With It?

Would Buchanan have risen to the highest office in the land if his peers honestly believed he was homosexual? It's hard to say. Today's perception is that 19th-century Americans were more homophobic than their 21st-century descendents. Yet in an era when sexuality stayed tucked beneath Victorian wraps, there was a de facto "don't ask, don't tell" policy for virtually any profession. Whatever their private proclivities, Buchanan and King clearly excelled in their public lives—at least until Buchanan got into the White House. Based on what little evidence history provides, neither man's sexual orientation had much, if any, bearing on what he accomplished, or failed to accomplish, in his career.

Paganini: 19th-Century Rock Star

Centuries before legendary bluesman Robert Johnson allegedly "stood at the crossroads" to sell his soul to the devil in return for uncanny abilities on the guitar, there was classical Genovese violinist Niccolo Paganini. Yet "classical" doesn't quite describe the mass hysteria his prowess provoked.

A child prodigy who played the mandolin with skill by age 5, Niccolo Paganini (1782–1840) took up the violin at 7 and gave his first public concert at 12. It wasn't long before he outpaced all of his potential teachers, so he began a regimen of his own construction that often ran more than 15 hours a day. Paganini's star soon rose at the royal court of Lucca, with successively more impressive appointments by Napoleon's sister, Elisa Baciocchi, Princess of Lucca. The violinist broke with the court soon enough, however, no doubt feeling stifled. By 1813, he had become a national sensation through a series of Milanese shows.

Calling All Groupies . . .

In 1828, Paganini embarked on a lengthy European tour, making him the first violinist to do so without backup musicians. He also memorized lengthy programs, never referring to sheet music onstage. He would cut the strings of his violin with scissors and perform complicated pieces on the single string that remained. He could tune a string so that it produced supernatural-sounding harmonies. People flocked to his shows, women fainted, and Paganini became a very wealthy man—the 19th-century equivalent of a modern-day rock star.

It was then, as his reputation grew, that some dubbed the master "Hexensohn," which means "witch's brat." It was speculated that he must have cut a deal with Lucifer, or perhaps was even the son of Satan himself. How else to explain such Paga-mania? The artist reveled in the rumors, sometimes inviting his mother to sit onstage, as if daring audience members to challenge his paternity. He took to wearing all black, often hiring a black carriage with four black horses to deliver him to theaters. But even before taking measures to accentuate it, he already presented an otherworldly appearance: Paganini was thin and pale with long black hair, a cadaverous face (major tooth loss) and eyes that rolled up inside his head as he played and swayed. He even had rock-star addictions— alcohol, women, and gambling. In fact, although he commanded the highest fees of any similar performer, he reportedly went bankrupt trying to open his own casino.

Playing to His Strengths

Research shows that Paganini may have had a genetic defect in collagen production now known as Ehlers-Danlos, resulting in joint hypermobility. He is also thought to have had Marfan's syndrome, a disorder of the connective tissue; symptoms include elongated facial features, limbs, and fingers. These disabilities were turned to his advantage: Paganini could play up to three octaves across the fret board without ever having to shift his hand.

Shunned in Death

On May 27, 1840, Paganini died in Nice, in present-day France, from larynx cancer. During his lifetime, he composed 24 caprices, a series of sonatas, and 6 violin con certos. Ironically, the reputation Paganini had so carefully cultivated literally followed him beyond death, with negative consequences. Not receiving final absolution—some say he even refused a priest who could have administered it—he was initially refused a Christian burial by the Catholic Church. Paganini's body was not buried in consecrated ground until five years after his death. One story claims his remains were stored in the family basement; a darker version has his son (by a mistress) traveling around Europe with the corpse until it was granted a decent resting place.

Whatever the case and however snubbed he was in death, the fame and intrigue of mythical proportions surrounding Paganini's life can be summed up in his quote, "I am not handsome, but when women hear me play, they come crawling to my feet." Hey, it's not boasting if it's true.

CHAPTER 7

LISTS: ODD, ABSURD, AND OTHERWISE

8 Quirky Festivals in North America

Looking for somewhere wacky to have a good time? Festivals, no matter how kooky, bring out the best in creativity. A festivalgoer can celebrate animals, insects, foods, historical events, and just about any other topic under the sun. It's easy to fill your calendar with events. Check out these examples.

1. Frozen Dead Guy Days (Nederland, Colorado)

The fun at the annual Frozen Dead Guy Days festival heats up Nederland during Colorado's typically frosty March. The fest commemorates a cryogenically-preserved Norwegian who has been kept in a shed by his grandson since 1994. Visitors are encouraged to come dressed as a frozen or dead character to a dance tagged "Grandpa's Blue Ball." Coffin races and a parade featuring antique hearses are among the liveliest attractions, along with salmon tossing and a frozen beach volleyball tournament. The event started in 2002 and annually attracts about 7,000 visitors.

2. Secret City Festival (Oak Ridge, Tennessee)

The annual Secret City Festival highlights the important role Oak Ridge played in World War II. In the 1940s, researchers there developed the top secret atomic bomb—hence the city's nickname—and today visitors can tour Manhattan Project sites to see where the bomb was devised. One of the country's largest World War II reenactments is also a popular draw, with roaring tanks, motorcycles, and other vintage military gear. Each June, the event draws about 20,000 people to Oak Ridge, which is nestled between the picturesque Cumberland and Great Smoky Mountains.

3. Nanaimo Marine Festival (Nanaimo, British Columbia)

At the Nanaimo Marine Festival held in mid-July, up to 200 "tubbers" compete in the Great International World Championship Bathtub Race across a 36-mile course. Using just about any conceivable watercraft, most of which at least vaguely resemble a bathtub, contestants must make it to Vancouver's Fisherman's Cove across the Straits of Georgia. The first race was held in 1967 and activities have expanded since to include a food fair, craft show, Kiddies' Karnival, and waiters' race.

4. BugFest (Raleigh, North Carolina)

Billed as the nation's largest single-day festival featuring insects, BugFest attracts around 25,000 people to Raleigh each September. The event started in 1997 and now covers beekeeping demonstrations, a flea circus, and roach races. The festival features many exhibits on insects, from live spiders and centipedes, to displays on how bugs see. At Café Insecta, festivalgoers can sample Buggy Bean

Dip with Crackers, Quivering Wax Worm Quiche, Stir-fried Cantonese Crickets over rice, and Three Bug Salad, among other aptly named goodies that actually include worms, ants, and related critters raised for cooking.

5. Rattlesnake Roundup (Freer, Texas)

Billed as the biggest party in Texas, the Freer Rattlesnake Roundup held each May features nationally known country and Tejano artists . . . and loads and loads of snakes. In addition to daredevil snake shows, snake twirling displays, a carnival, arts and crafts, and fried rattlesnake to chaw, prizes are given out for the longest and smallest rattlesnakes, and for the most nonvenomous snakes brought to the fest by one person.

6. Barnesville Potato Days (Barnesville, Minnesota)

Up to 14,000 visitors head to west-central Minnesota for Barnesville Potato Days in late August when this small town celebrates the lowly spud with a great menu of activities. The Potato Salad Cook-off attracts onlookers eager to compare the year's winning recipe with how Grandma used to make this popular picnic dish. Things can get messy during mashed potato wrestling, but the Miss Tator Tot pageant is much more refined. Of course, there is plenty of food to sample, including Norwegian *lefse*, potato pancakes, potato sausage, potato soup, and traditional German potato dumplings. On Friday, there's even a free French Fry Feed. Barnesville, tucked away in the fertile Red River Valley, has been honoring the crop of choice of many nearby farmers with this festival since 1938.

7. Faux Film Festival (Portland, Oregon)

For anyone who loves fake commercials or movie trailers, Portland's Faux Film Festival is the ticket to a surreal never-never land. Mockumentaries and other celluloid spoofs are among the dozens of goofy entries shown in the historic 460-seat Hollywood Theatre. Past viewings have included the silly classic, *It Came from the Lint Trap* and the quirky *The Lady from Sockholm*, a film noir featuring sock puppets. The fest is usually staged at the end of March, with a packed house at each screening.

8. Contraband Days Pirate Festival (Lake Charles, Louisiana)

Legend has it that buccaneer Jean Lafitte buried an enormous treasure somewhere along Lake Charles's sandy shoreline. Since 1958, Contraband Days Pirate Festival, which attracts more than 100,000 people, has been honoring the legend each May. Perhaps one of the funniest sights of the festival is when the mayor is made to walk the plank after pirates take over the town. The plucky civic chief is naturally rescued quickly, then is free to enjoy the rest of the fest with its carnival, arm wrestling competition, sailboat regatta, and bed races. With an eclectic selection of nearly 100 different events, Contraband Days is frequently chosen by the American Bus Association as a Top 100 Event in North America.

7 Bizarre Foreign Vehicle Names

1. Nissan Fairlady Z; Japan, 1970–Present
2. Flirt; Italy, 1913–1914
3. Humber Super Snipe; Great Britain, 1946–1967

4. Wartburg Knight; East Germany, 1966–1990
5. Geely PU; China, 2006
6. Beijing Jinggangshan; China, 1958–1960
7. Dri-Sleeve Moonraker; Great Britain, 1971–1972

27 Phobias and Their Definitions

1. Ablutophobia: Fear of washing or bathing
2. Acrophobia: Fear of heights
3. Agoraphobia: Fear of open spaces, crowds, or leaving a safe place
4. Ailurophobia: Fear of cats
5. Alektorophobia: Fear of chickens
6. Anthropophobia: Fear of people
7. Anuptaphobia: Fear of staying single
8. Arachnophobia: Fear of spiders
9. Atychiphobia: Fear of failure
10. Autophobia: Fear of oneself or of being alone
11. Aviophobia: Fear of flying
12. Caligynephobia: Fear of beautiful women
13. Coulrophobia: Fear of clowns
14. Cynophobia: Fear of dogs
15. Gamophobia: Fear of marriage
16. Ichthyophobia: Fear of fish
17. Melanophobia: Fear of the color black
18. Mysophobia: Fear of germs or dirt
19. Nyctophobia: Fear of the dark or of night
20. Ophidiophobia/Herpetophobia: Fear of snakes
21. Ornithophobia: Fear of birds
22. Phasmophobia/Spectrophobia: Fear of ghosts
23. Philophobia: Fear of being in love
24. Photophobia: Fear of light
25. Pupaphobia: Fear of puppets
26. Pyrophobia: Fear of fire
27. Thanatophobia or Thantophobia: Fear of death or dying

12 Items at a Feast of Henry VIII

Henry VIII, who ruled England from 1509 until his death in 1547, was known for his voracious appetite. Portraits of Henry show a man almost as wide as he was tall. When he wasn't marrying, divorcing, or beheading his wives (he was on his sixth marriage when he died at age 58), this medieval ruler dined like a glutton. He enjoyed banquets so much that he extended the kitchen of Hampton Court Palace to fill 55 rooms. The 200 members of the kitchen staff provided meals of up to 14 courses for the 600 people in the king's court. Here are some dishes served at a typical feast.

1. Spit-Roasted Meat

Spit-roasted meat—usually a pig or boar—was eaten at every meal. It was an expression of extreme wealth because only the rich could afford fresh meat year-round; only the very rich could afford to roast it, since this required much more fuel than boiling; and only the super-wealthy could pay a "spit boy" to turn the spit all day. In a typical year, the royal kitchen served 1,240 oxen, 8,200 sheep, 2,330 deer, 760 calves, 1,870 pigs, and 53 wild boar. That's more than 14,000 large animals, meaning each member of the court was consuming about 23 animals every year.

2. Grilled Beavers' Tails

These tasty morsels were particularly popular on Fridays, when, according to Christian tradition, it was forbidden to eat meat. Rather conveniently, medieval people classified beavers as fish.

3. Whale Meat

Another popular dish for Fridays, whale meat was fairly common and cheap, due to the plentiful supply of whales in the North Sea, each of which could feed hundreds of people. It was typically served boiled or very well roasted.

4. Whole Roasted Peacock

This delicacy was served dressed in its own iridescent blue feathers (which were plucked, then replaced after the bird had been cooked), with its beak gilded in gold leaf.

5. Internal Organs

If you're squeamish, stop reading now. Medieval cooks didn't believe in wasting any part of an animal, and, in fact, internal organs were often regarded as delicacies. Beef lungs, spleen, and even udders were considered fit for a king and were usually preserved in brine or vinegar.

6. Black Pudding

Another popular dish—still served in parts of England—was black pudding. This sausage is made by filling a length of pig's intestine with the animal's boiled, congealed blood.

7. Boar's Head

A boar's head, garnished with bay and rosemary, served as the centerpiece of Christmas feasts. It certainly outdoes a floral display.

8. Roasted Swan

Roasted swan was another treat reserved for special occasions, largely because swans were regarded as too noble and dignified for everyday consumption. The bird was often presented to the table with a gold crown upon its head. To this day, English law stipulates that all mute swans are owned by the Crown and may not be eaten without permission from the Queen.

9. Vegetables

Perhaps the only type of food Henry and his court didn't consume to excess was vegetables, which were viewed as the food of the poor and made up less than 20 percent of the royal diet.

10. Marzipan

A paste made from ground almonds, sugar, and egg whites and flavored with cinnamon and pepper, marzipan was occasionally served at the end of a meal, although desserts weren't popular in England until the 18th century when incredibly elaborate sugar sculptures became popular among the aristocracy.

11. Spiced Fruitcake

The exception to the no dessert rule was during the Twelfth Night banquet on January 6, when a special spiced fruitcake containing a dried pea (or bean) was served. Whoever found the pea would be king or queen of the pea (or bean) and was treated as a guest of honor for the remainder of the evening.

12. Wine and Ale

All this food was washed down with enormous quantities of wine and ale. Historians estimate that 600,000 gallons of ale (enough to fill an Olympic-size swimming pool) and around 75,000 gallons of wine (enough to fill 1,500 bathtubs) were drunk every year at Hampton Court Palace.

9 Strange Last Wills and Testaments

A will is supposed to help surviving family and friends dispose of your estate after you've passed away. Many people use it as an opportunity to send a message from beyond the grave, either by punishing potential heirs with nothing or perhaps by giving away something fun or unusual to remember them by. Where there's a will, there's a way, so make sure you have a good will before you go away for good.

1. Harry Houdini

Harry Houdini, born in 1874, was considered the greatest magician and escape artist of his era, and possibly of all time. When he died in 1926 from a ruptured appendix, Houdini left his magician's equipment to his brother Theodore, his former partner who performed under the name Hardeen. His library of books on magic and the occult was offered to the American Society for Psychical Research on the condition that J. Malcolm Bird, research officer and editor of the *ASPR Journal*, resign. Bird refused and the collection went instead to the Library of Congress. The rabbits he pulled out of his hat went to the children of friends. Houdini left his wife a secret code—ten words chosen at random—that he would use to contact her from the afterlife. His wife held annual séances on Halloween for ten years after his death, but Houdini never appeared.

2. Marie Curie

Born in Russian-occupied Poland in 1867, Marie Curie moved to Paris at age 24 to study science. As a physicist and chemist, Madame Curie was a pioneer in the early field of radioactivity, later becoming the first two-time Nobel laureate and the only person to win Nobel Prizes in two different fields of science—physics and chemistry. When she died in 1934, a gram of pure radium, originally received as a gift from the women of America, was her only property of substantial worth. Her will stated: "The value of the element being too great to transfer to a personal heritage, I desire to will the gram of radium to the University of Paris on the condition that my daughter, Irene Curie, shall have entire liberty to use this gram . . . according to the conditions under which her scientific researches shall be pursued." Element 96, Curium (Cm), was named in honor of Marie and her husband, Pierre.

3. William Randolph Hearst

Multimillionaire newspaper magnate William Randolph Hearst was born in San Francisco in 1863. When he died in 1951, in accordance with his will, his $59.5 million estate was divided into three trusts—one each for his widow, sons, and the Hearst Foundation for Charitable Purposes. Challenging those who claimed he had children out of wedlock, Hearst willed anyone who could prove "that he or she is a child of mine . . . the sum of one dollar. I hereby declare that any such asserted claim . . . would be utterly false." No one claimed it. The book-length will included the disposition of his $30 million castle near San Simeon, California. The University of California could have had it but decided it was too expensive to maintain, so the state government took it, and it is now a state and national historic landmark open for public tours.

4. Jonathan Jackson

Animal lover Jonathan Jackson died around 1880. His will stipulated that: "It is man's duty as lord of animals to watch over and protect the lesser and feebler." So he left money for the creation of a cat house—a place where cats could enjoy comforts such as bedrooms, a dining hall, an auditorium to listen to live accordion music, an exercise room, and a specially designed roof for climbing without risking any of their nine lives.

5. S. Sanborn

When S. Sanborn, an American hatmaker, died in 1871, he left his body to science, bequeathing it to Oliver Wendell Holmes, Sr., (then a professor of anatomy at Harvard Medical School) and one of Holmes's colleagues. The will stipulated that two drums were to be made out of Sanborn's skin and given to a friend on the condition that every June 17 at dawn he would pound out the tune "Yankee Doodle" at Bunker Hill to commemorate the anniversary of the famous Revolutionary War battle. The rest of his body was "to be composted for a fertilizer to contribute to the growth of an American elm, to be planted in some rural thoroughfare."

6. John Bowman

Vermont tanner John Bowman believed that after his death, he, his dead wife, and two daughters would be reincarnated together. When he died in 1891, his will provided a $50,000 trust fund for the maintenance of his 21-room mansion and mausoleum. The will required servants to serve dinner every night just in case the Bowmans were hungry when they returned from the dead. This stipulation was carried out until 1950, when the trust money ran out.

7. James Kidd

James Kidd, an Arizona hermit and miner, disappeared in 1949 and was legally declared dead in 1956. His handwritten will was found in 1963 and stipulated that his $275,000 estate should "go in a research for some scientific proof of a soul of a human body which leaves at death." More than 100 petitions for the inheritance were dismissed by the court. In 1971, the money was awarded to the American Society for Psychical Research in New York City, although it failed to prove the soul's existence.

8. Eleanor E. Ritchey

Eleanor E. Ritchey, heiress to the Quaker State Refining Corporation, passed on her $4.5 million fortune to her 150 dogs when she died in Florida in 1968. The will was contested, and in 1973 the dogs received $9 million. By the time the estate was finally settled its value had jumped to $14 million but only 73 of the dogs were still alive. When the last dog died in 1984, the remainder of the estate went to the Auburn University Research Foundation for research into animal diseases.

9. Janis Joplin

Janis Joplin was born in Port Arthur, Texas, on January 19, 1943. In her brief career as a rock and blues singer, she recorded four albums containing a number of rock classics, including "Piece of My Heart," "To Love Somebody," and "Me and Bobby McGee." Known for her heavy drinking and drug use, she died of an overdose on October 4, 1970. Janis made changes to her will just two days before her death. She set aside $2,500 to pay for a posthumous all-night party for 200 guests at her favorite pub in San Anselmo, California, "so my friends can get blasted after I'm gone." The bulk of her estate reportedly went to her parents.

16 Unusual Book Titles

1. *How to Avoid Huge Ships* by John W. Trimmer
2. *Scouts in Bondage* by Michael Bell
3. *Be Bold with Bananas* by Crescent Books
4. *Fancy Coffins to Make Yourself* by Dale L. Power
5. *The Flat-Footed Flies of Europe* by Peter J. Chandler
6. *101 Uses for an Old Farm Tractor* by Michael Dregni
7. *Across Europe by Kangaroo* by Joseph R. Barry
8. *101 Super Uses for Tampon Applicators* by Lori Katz and Barbara Meyer
9. *Suture Self* by Mary Daheim
10. *The Making of a Moron* by Niall Brennan
11. *How to Make Love While Conscious* by Guy Kettelhack
12. *Underwater Acoustics Handbook* by Vernon Martin Albers
13. *Superfluous Hair and Its Removal* by A. F. Niemoeller
14. *Lightweight Sandwich Construction* by J. M. Davies

15. *The Devil's Cloth: A History of Stripes* by
    Michel Pastoureaut
16. *How to Be a Pope: What to Do and Where to Go
    Once You're in the Vatican* by Piers Marchant

9 Odd Things
Insured by Lloyds of London

Average people insure average things like cars, houses, and maybe even a boat. Celebrities insure legs, voices, and some things you might not want to examine if you're a claims adjuster. Here are a few unusual things insured by the famous Lloyds of London over the years.

1. In 1957, world-famous food critic Egon Ronay wrote and published the first edition of *Egon Ronay's Guide to British Eateries*. Because his endorsement could make or break a restaurant, Ronay insured his taste buds for $400,000.

2. In the 1940s, executives at 20th Century Fox had the legs of actress Betty Grable insured for $1 million each. After taking out the policies, Grable probably wished she had added a rider to protect her from injury while the insurance agents fought over who would inspect her when making a claim.

3. While playing on Australia's national cricket team from 1985 to 1994, Merv Hughes took out an estimated $370,000 policy on his trademark walrus mustache, which, combined with his 6' 4" physique and outstanding playing ability, made him one of the most recognized cricketers in the world.

4. Representing the Cheerio Yo-Yo Company of Canada, 13-year-old Harvey Lowe won the 1932 World Yo-Yo championships in London and toured Europe from 1932 to 1935. He even taught Edward VIII, the Prince of Wales, how to yo-yo. Lowe was so valuable to Cheerio that the company insured his hands for $150,000.

5. From 1967 to 1992, British comedian and singer Ken Dodd was in *The Guinness Book of Records* for the world's longest joke-telling session—1,500 jokes in three and a half hours. Dodd has sold more than 100 million comedy records and is famous for his frizzy hair, ever-present feather duster, and extremely large buckteeth. His teeth are so important to his act that Dodd had them insured for $7.4 million, surely making his insurance agent grin.

6. During the height of his career, Michael Flatley—star of *Riverdance* and *Lord of the Dance*—insured his legs for an unbelievable $47 million. Before becoming the world's most famous Irish step dancer, the Chicago native trained as a boxer and won the Golden Gloves Championship in 1975, undoubtedly dazzling his opponents with some extremely fast and fancy footwork.

7. The famous comedy team of Bud Abbott and Lou Costello seemed to work extremely well together, especially in their famous "Who's on First?" routine. But to protect against a career-ending argument, they took out a $250,000 insurance policy over a five-year period. After more than 20 years together, the team split up in 1957—not due to a disagreement, but because the Internal Revenue Service got them for back taxes, which forced them to sell many of their assets, including the rights to their many films.

8. Rock and Roll Hall of Famer Bruce Springsteen is known to his fans as The Boss, but Springsteen knows that he could be demoted to part-time status with one case of laryngitis. That's why in the 1980s he insured his famous gravelly voice for $6 million. Rod Stewart has also insured his throat and Bob Dylan his vocal cords to protect themselves from that inevitable day when they stop blowin' in the wind.

9. Before rock, a popular type of music in England in the 1950s was skiffle, a type of folk music with a jazz and blues influence played on washboards, jugs, kazoos, and cigar-box fiddles. It was so big at the time that a washboard player named Chas McDevitt tried to protect his career by insuring his fingers for $9,300. It didn't do him much good because skiffle was replaced by rock 'n' roll, washboards by washing machines, and McDevitt by McCartney.

18 Odd Items for Sale in Japanese Vending Machines

Japan seems to have a yen for selling unusual products via vending machine—they sell more than any other country. Aside from the usual candy, gum, and cigarettes, here are some of the more obscure items available for purchase in Japanese vending machines.

1. Fresh eggs
2. Bags of rice in various sizes
3. Fishing line, fish hooks, and fish bait
4. Toilet paper in small packets—most public restrooms in Japan charge a fee for toilet paper
5. Fresh flowers
6. Frequent flyer miles—Japan Air Lines (JAL) has a machine that reads a credit card and boarding pass and issues frequent flyer miles
7. Beer in cans or two-liter jugs
8. Film and disposable cameras
9. Pornographic magazines
10. Designer condoms
11. Batteries
12. Live rhinoceros beetles—a popular pet for Japanese children
13. Kerosene—for home space heaters
14. Dry ice—sold at supermarkets for keeping frozen food cold until the customer gets home
15. Sake in preheated containers
16. Cups of hot noodles
17. Fortunes—found at shrines and temples
18. Umbrellas—for both rain and shade

11 Stupid Legal Warnings

Our lawsuit-obsessed society has forced product manufacturers to cover their you-know-whats by writing
warning labels to protect us from ourselves. Some are
funny, some are absolutely ridiculous, but all are guaran-
teed to stand up in court.

1. Child-size Superman and Batman costumes come
   with this warning label: "Wearing of this garment does
   not enable you to fly."
2. A clothes iron comes with this caution: "Warning:
   Never iron clothes on the body." Ouch!
3. The instructions for a medical thermometer advise:
   "Do not use orally after using rectally."
4. The side of a Slush Puppy cup warns: "This ice may
   be cold." (The only thing dumber than this would be
   a disclaimer stating: "No puppies were harmed in the
   making of this product.")
5. The box of a 500-piece puzzle reads: "Some
   assembly required."
6. A Power Puff Girls costume discourages: "You cannot
   save the world!"
7. A box of PMS relief tablets has this advice: "Warning:
   Do not use if you have prostate problems."
8. Cans of Easy Cheese contain this instruction: "For best
   results, remove cap."
9. A warning label on a nighttime sleep-aid reads:
   "Warning: May cause drowsiness."
10. Cans of self-defense pepper spray caution:
    "May irritate eyes."
11. Both boys and girls should read the label on the
    Harry Potter toy broom: "This broom does not
    actually fly."

CHAPTER 8

CATS, DOGS, AND BEYOND

Dressed to the Nines

Why on earth would people dress up their pets? On the practical side, certain breeds of dogs don't have enough meat on their bones or fur in their coats to keep themselves warm in cold weather, so you can buy little coats or wraps to help them stay warm. Of course, you can also buy your dog a bathing suit, though there's no physiological need for it. Indeed, websites sell thousands of doggie Halloween costumes—from pirates to princesses, Superman to Darth Vader. And this brings us to the psychological part of the equation. Many people consider a pet to be a member of the family, which helps explain why Americans spend tens of billions of dollars per year on their animals.

What other reasons might we have for putting capes on our dogs or Santa Claus hats on our cats? One study suggests that it may be because we are lonely. In research conducted at the University of Chicago, 99 people were asked to describe their own pet or the pet of someone they knew. The lonelier the people were in their everyday lives, the more likely they were to use human traits to describe their pets, employing such words as "thoughtful" and "sympathetic."

The lesson? We are social creatures, and when the need to connect with other humans is not fulfilled, we seek out ways to fill the void. For some of us, Mr. Fluffy clad in a woolly sweater fits the bill.

The Restless Lives of Fish

It's hard to tell whether fish are sleeping because they don't have eyelids. That's why you'll never win a staring contest with your pet guppy—its eyes are always open.

Since fish can't close their eyes, how do they get their beauty sleep? They don't, at least not in the way we humans do. Their body functions slow down and they get a bit dozy, but they're generally still alert enough to scatter when danger arises. You could say that they're having a relaxing daydream, but they never actually fall into a deep sleep.

Some fish simply float motionless in the water as they doze; others, such as grouper and rockfish, rest against rocks or plants. The craftier varieties, like bass and perch, hole up underneath rocks and logs or hide in crevices. Others stay on the move while in a daze, recharging without ever stopping.

In the 1930s, biologist David Graham watched a fish sleeping upright on its tail for an hour or so. Then Graham turned on the lights, and the fish jerked back into a swimming position and darted around. It was the aquatic equivalent of being caught napping in school.

When exactly do fish rest? It varies from species to species. Most fish rely on the weak light from the surface to see, and since that light pretty much disappears at night, it's thought that a lot of fish do their resting then. However, some fish rest during the day, while others do so randomly. There are, it seems, no set bedtimes in the fish world.

Your Pet Goldfish
Just Might Save Your Life

Research shows that gazing into a fish-filled aquarium can help to reduce a person's stress, at least temporarily. That's why there are fish tanks in the waiting rooms of many medical and dental offices.

In the 1980s, researchers at the University of Pennsylvania found that watching fish in an aquarium is far more effective at reducing stress than watching an aquarium without fish. In 1999, Nancy Edwards, a professor of nursing at Purdue University, discovered that Alzheimer's patients who were exposed to fish-filled aquariums were more relaxed and alert and even began to eat a healthier diet. Another study showed that exposure to aquariums can contribute to decreased stress and hyperactivity among people who suffer from attention deficit hyperactivity disorder, or ADHD. Nobody is sure exactly why fish are so calming. The Purdue University study theorized that the combination of movement, color, and sound in an aquarium has a relaxing effect.

But it's not just fish that help reduce stress. Having a pet of any kind leads to better health. A 2007 study at Queen's University in Belfast, Northern Ireland, showed that dog owners tended to have lower blood pressure and cholesterol than people who didn't own dogs. The study proposed that pet owners in general are healthier than the population on average and also suggested that having a dog is better for you than having a cat. However, the study didn't weigh in on how dogs and cats compare to fish.

Out of Sight, Out of Mind

If you think a cat isn't smart, consider that it's the only animal with enough sense to bury its waste. Technically, cats aren't the only animals that bury their waste. We humans have been burying our bodily waste for thousands of years, and all signs point toward the continuance of this habit. Civilizations would be overrun by stink if we didn't. But in terms of "lower" animals, cats are indeed the only animals that have the courtesy to dispose of their droppings. The only other animal that possesses an inclination to do something special with its feces is the chimpanzee, which will sometimes chuck turds at rival chimps in fits of anger. Every other animal just lets the turds fall where they will.

Uncovering the Origins

The house cat's habit of covering its feces probably goes back to its ancestors in the wild. In nature, cats sometimes bury their waste in an effort to hide it from predators and rival cats. In effect, it's the opposite of using urine to mark territory; in an effort to remain incognito, cats do their best to hide any trace of their presence.

By the same token, a dominant cat will leave its poop anywhere it pleases within its territory in order to scare off trespassing felines. A pile of fly-covered waste, and the distinctive smell that wafts from that pile, functions like a BEWARE OF CAT sign. For another cat to ignore this warning would be to invite trouble in the form of teeth and claws.

Your house cat's tendency to bury its feces in a litter box may be a sign that it recognizes your dominance in the house. And if it uses the litter box but neglects to cover its leavings—as some cats do—it may be your tabby's way of acknowledging a kind of shared dominance over the abode.

You needn't worry about your place in the pecking order until you come home and find urine stains in the corners of the room and feces in the middle of the floor. At that point, you are trespassing on your cat's territory—sitting on *its* couch, watching *its* television, popping *its* popcorn—and you'd better start paying rent . . . or prepare to face the terrible wrath of the tabby cat.

A Snack of Convenience

There's no denying that cats have a thing for mice. It begins with the thrill of the chase, and if all goes as planned (for the cat), it ends with the satisfaction of downing a wiggling bundle of fur and bones, squeak and all.

It's feline instinct, but it's not entirely unlike the way you hit the couch, reach for the remote control, turn on the television, enjoy the thrill of a cop-show chase, and stuff your face with those special potato chips—the cheap, greasy ones that you'd never admit to loving. What's the similarity? For both the cat and for you, it's the easiest thing that's available because it's right in front of you. It's low-hanging fruit, so to speak.

If a mouse is so brazen or so foolish as to wander into Tabby's territory, the cat is going to make entertainment and a snack out of it. If that television is just going to sit there and if those chips are simply going to take up cupboard space, your best option is to make entertainment and a snack out of them. You get the general idea, right?

A cat would rather dine on, say, a tuna, but there aren't any flopping around your family rec room. Mice, on the other hand, are plentiful. Remember, cats also dine on bugs—and you don't see bug-flavored cat food at your local pet store, do you?

Six Pets That Traveled Long Distances to Get Home

Salmon follow the smell of their home waters. Birds and bees appear to navigate by the sun, stars, and moon. We can't really explain how so many lost dogs and cats magically seem to find their way back to their owners over great distances, so we'll just tell you about them instead.

1. **Emily the cat went across the pond:** Lesley and Donny McElhiney's home in Appleton, Wisconsin, wasn't the same after their one-year-old tabby Emily disappeared. But she didn't just disappear, she went on a 4,500-mile adventure! It seems Emily was on her evening prowl when she found herself on a truck to Chicago inside a container of paper bales. From there she was shipped to Belgium, finally arriving in France where employees at a laminating company found her thin and thirsty. Since she was wearing tags, it didn't take

long for Emily to be reunited with her family, compliments of Continental Airlines.

2. **Howie the Persian cat crossed the Australian outback:** The Hicks family wanted their cat to be lovingly cared for while they went on an extended vacation overseas. So, they took him to stay with relatives who lived more than 1,000 miles away. Months later, when they returned to retrieve Howie, they were told that he had run away. The Hicks were distraught, assuming that because Howie was an indoor cat, he wouldn't have the survival skills to make it on his own. A year later, their daughter returned home from school one day and saw a mangy, unkempt, and starving cat. Yep, it was Howie. It had taken him 12 months to cross 1,000 miles of Australian outback, but Howie had come home.

3. **Tony the mutt finds his family:** When the Doolen family of Aurora, Illinois, moved to East Lansing, Michigan, nearly 260 miles away, they gave away their mixed-breed dog Tony. Six weeks later, who came trotting down the street in East Lansing and made himself known to Mr. Doolen? That's right—Tony. Doolen recognized a notch on Tony's collar that he'd cut while still living in Illinois.

4. **Madonna heads to the massage parlor:** Now here's a finicky cat! This seven-year-old tabby moved from Kitchener, Ontario, with her owner Nina in order to start a new branch of the family massage parlor business. Their new home base was Windsor, but within weeks, Madonna was nowhere to be found. She eventually showed up at her original massage

parlor, where Nina's sister was the new proprietor. Total walking distance? About 150 miles.

5. Troubles finds his way through ten miles of jungle: Troubles, a scout dog, and his handler William Richardson were taken via helicopter deep into the war zone in South Vietnam in the late 1960s. When Richardson was wounded by enemy fire and taken to a hospital, Troubles was abandoned by the rest of the unit. Three weeks later, Troubles showed up at his home at the First Air Cavalry Division Headquarters in An Khe, South Vietnam. But he wouldn't let any one near him—he was on a mission! Troubles searched the tents and eventually curled up for a nap after he found a pile of Richardson's clothes to use for a bed.

6. Misele the farm cat goes to the hospital: When 82-year-old Alfonse Mondry was taken to a hospital in France, his cat Misele missed him greatly. So she took off and walked across cattle fields, rock quarries, forests, and busy highways. She entered the hospital—where she had never been before—and found her owner's room. The nurses called the doctor right away when they found Mondry resting comfortably with his cat purring on his lap.

Extreme Pet Pampering

They're man's best friend, sure—but $12 million for a dog? Hotel heiress Leona Helmsley made her priorities clear when she left a large chunk of her family fortune to her pooch. A court ultimately intervened, reducing the canine's inheritance to a measly $2 million and redistributing the rest to Helmsley's charitable foundation. Still, a nearly $200,000 annual budget isn't bad for an animal. As it turns out, dogs living, well, high on the dog is not as unusual as one might think.

The Fashion

Plenty of pet owners are providing the high life for Fido. America's pet spending tops $40 billion a year—double what we're shelling out for children's toys. Some dogs are even amassing enormous accessory collections. Designer carriers made by companies such as Juicy Couture can go for nearly $300 a pop. Jewelers are marketing pricey dog-collar charms made of real sapphires and pearls. There are perfume-scented leashes, fashionable doggy shoes, and specially designed dog sunglasses. Add the fabulous outfits—complete with sweaters, pajamas, and even hats—and Fido is one must-see pup. But it doesn't stop at material possessions.

The Relaxation

Animal spas all over the country offer services such as facials for cats and dogs. There are massages, acupuncture, and even cosmetic surgeries on the menu. Hotels such as Manhattan's Ritzy Canine Carriage House offer animal suites at $80 a night for large dogs. They can also get an hour-long massage for $60, and the hotel also offers grooming, training, a designer gift boutique, and room service. Other centers, such as the Inn's Naples Dog Center in Florida, provide special treatments that purportedly soothe an animal's emotional and spiritual state. Some spas even have pet herbal rinses, mud baths, swimming sessions, and surfing lessons for owners willing to splurge on their furry friend.

The Drinks

Tired of drinking alone? Now your four-legged friend can cozy up to the bar with you. Happy Tail Ale is a nonalcoholic brew made for dogs. It's noncarbonated and boasts all-natural beef drippings. Yum.

Perhaps your pet isn't bent on beer. How about fine wine? Bark Vineyards has built a business out of gourmet wine for cats and dogs. Also alcohol-free, the popular drink includes such flavors as "Barkundy," "Sauvignon Bark," "Pino Leasheo," and "White Sniff 'N' Tail." Really.

The Food

What good are all the drinkable delights without some fancy food to accompany them? Companies such as Evanger's offer up organic meal creations that seem fit for a five-star restaurant. For an extra fee, your pet can opt for kosher meals instead.

Sounds pretty good, doesn't it? Well, don't be jealous: You can share your dog's dishes. Dick Van Patten's Natural Balance Dog Food is made for both dog and human consumption. Just think: Now you can enjoy chili or a Chinese entrée right alongside your precious widdle snookums.

The Electronics

People aren't the only ones who can enjoy electronics. Gadgets such as the Talking Bone allow you to record messages for your pet that it can play when you aren't around. Meanwhile, the Pet Spa Grooming Machine gives them a spa treatment at home, complete with aromatherapy. You can also buy CDs to expose your animals to foreign languages. Perhaps best of all, though, Edible Greeting Cards creates holiday messages for animals that can be eaten. Creative and convenient!

One thing's for sure: The pet-pampering industry is a booming business, and many pet owners are more than willing to dish out the dough. Heck, if people are spending more on their Chihuahuas than their children, then maybe the hotel heiress wasn't as crazy as she seemed.

On second thought . . .

Why Did the Dog Pee on the Fire Hydrant? Because It Was There

And because it provided a handy way for the canine to mark its territory.

Dogs and people, animal behavior specialists claim, are more similar than we might think. Indeed, man shares a number of characteristics with his best friend. They're both creatures of habit. They both enjoy being petted. And they both pee on everything in sight. Okay, maybe not the last one. Usually.

But even if humans don't urinate on fire hydrants, the urge that causes dogs to do so is rooted in a trait humans and canines do share: territoriality. In suburban neighborhoods across the land, picket and chain-link fences border our yards, signaling to our neighbors, "This is my turf." Dogs, however, can't build fences, so they use what they have available to them: a seemingly never-ending supply of urine. By spraying everything in the vicinity, dogs stake their claim in the neighborhood land grab.

Urinating also serves as a form of canine communication. When a dog raises its leg at a fire hydrant, it's announcing to other dogs in the area, "Fido was here"—much like the way humans spray graffiti or carve their initials into public property.

Why fire hydrants? Actually, fire hydrants are only some of many objects dogs enjoy peeing on. Fire hydrants, trees, mailbox posts—virtually anything with a wide enough surface to retain a scent is a potential victim. It's possible the cliché of the fire hydrant stems from the fact that in many areas, fire hydrants are common and accessible targets. The fact that dogs are the traditional mascot, of firefighters may also be a reason.

The next time one of your neighbors erects an enormous fence around his or her yard, don't get upset—be grateful. Consider the alternative.

CHAPTER 9

LOVE: IT'S COMPLICATED

Why Spouses Start to Look Alike

Have you ever met a married couple that looked so alike you could have sworn they were brother and sister? Well, scientific research has come up with a few explanations as to why.

Compatibility Counts

For starters, it seems that we seek out mates who have features that are similar to our own. Recent studies suggest that we're attracted to those who look like us because they tend to have comparable personalities.

It's often said that women "marry their fathers." Research at the University of Pécs in Hungary supports this notion. Women tend to choose husbands who resemble their natural fathers—even if they're adopted. Scientists characterize it as "sexual imprinting," and it's known to occur in many animal species. Glenn Weisfeld, a human ethologist at Wayne State University in Detroit, says that there seems to be an advantage to selecting mates who are similar to ourselves: "Fortuitous genetic combinations" are retained in our offspring.

This doesn't give you carte blanche to marry your cute first cousin Betty. When it comes to mating, it's best to avoid people who are members of your family tree. But it doesn't hurt to pick a guy or gal who shares your dark features or toothy smile. Studies show that partners who are genetically similar to each other tend to have happier marriages.

Togetherness

It seems the longer couples stay together, the more their likenesses grow. A study by Robert Zajonc, a psychologist at the University of Michigan, found this to be the case—even among couples who didn't particularly look alike when they first got hitched. In Zajonc's study, people were presented with random photographs of men's and women's faces and asked to match up couples according to resemblance. Half of the photos were individual shots of couples that were taken when they were first married; the other half were individual shots of the same couples after twenty-five years of wedlock.

What do you know? People were able to match up husbands and wives far more often when looking at photographs of the couples when they were older than when they were younger. It seems with time, the couples' similarities became much more discernible. Why? Zajonc says husbands and wives start looking like each other because they spend decades sharing the same life experiences and emotions. Spouses often mimic the facial expressions of each other as a sign of empathy and closeness. Think of that the next time you and your spouse exchange smiles, sighs, or looks of contempt. Before you know it, you'll be sharing a life complete with matching facial sagging and wrinkle patterns! Hey, it's better than being told you look like your dog.

Love at First Sight

It happens all the time in Hollywood, but in the real world, instant fireworks between two people rarely go off.

Here Are the Facts, Romeo

Your eyes meet from across a crowded room—shazam! Sparks fly. Fireworks explode. In an instant, you both know that you have found the missing piece to your puzzle. You are the yin to his yang. She is the chocolate to your peanut butter.

At least that's usually how it goes in those corny chick flicks. What about in real life? Can two strangers simply lock looks and spontaneously combust into an epic romance, just like Romeo and Juliet, Scarlett and Rhett, and Dharma and Greg?

Not to be unromantic, but relationship researchers say that love at first sight is rare. Only 11 percent of couples in one interview study said that they had fallen in love at first glance. The survey—conducted by social psychologist Ayala Malach Pines, author of *Falling in Love: Why We Choose the Lovers We Choose*—also revealed that more couples, one-third of them, said they fell in love gradually.

But who wants to watch a movie about a guy and a girl cautiously getting to know one another over a couple hundred soy lattes? It's much more exciting to see—and feel—a fiery spark of desire. Maybe that's why some people seem to stray into the trap of falling in love at first sight over and over again.

Love vs. Lust

Remember Pepé Le Pew from the Looney Tunes cartoons? In search of *l'amour*, he falls at the sight of Penelope in almost every episode. It goes to show that there's a difference between love at first sight and lust at first leer. Penelope isn't even the "petite femme skunk" Pepé thinks she is—she's a black cat with a white stripe painted down her back. In other words: not a suitable life partner.

Hey, sometimes the eyes see what they want to see (especially when they're wearing beer goggles). Interestingly, when this kind of instantaneous physical attraction strikes, it's usually the guys who fall prey to it. In their defense, evolutionary psychologist David Buss says that in a biological sense, this is perfectly logical. Buss's research suggests that a man is taken by the physical appearance of a woman because it gives him cues about her fertility and reproductive value. From an evolutionary standpoint, love at first sight enabled early men and women to spot each other and start breeding straight away.

In today's context, researchers in Scotland at the University of Aberdeen's Face Research Lab say that love at first sight might exist, but it's more about ego and sex than love and romance. So forget what you saw in that Lifetime movie. To put it plainly: People are attracted to those who are attracted to them. Hey, baby—do you believe in love at first sight, or should I walk by again?

The Six Wives of Henry VIII

History has much to say about England's King Henry VIII (1491–1547) and his six wives. Henry was certainly the marrying type, yet he held no qualms about ending a marriage that inconvenienced him. How he ended those marriages is where historical fact blurs into misconceptions. Many people believe that as Henry lost interest in his wives, they lost their heads on the executioner's block.

But Henry wasn't quite the lady killer he's perceived to be. In actuality, two of Henry's wives survived their marriage to him, and only two were beheaded. Here's a brief look at how things really ended between Henry and his brides.

Catherine of Aragon (1485–1536): married 1509, divorced 1533. Catherine of Aragon proved to be the most tormented of Henry's wives. It didn't help that she wasn't considered attractive, but she was doomed by her inability to provide Henry with a male heir (their only surviving child, Mary, would later establish her own blood-stained reign). Catherine suffered through Henry's scorn, neglect, and public infidelities, most notably with her eventual successor in the royal marital bed, Anne Boleyn.

By 1526, desperate for a son and smitten by Anne, Henry began his ultimately unsuccessful petitioning of Pope Clement VII for an annulment from Catherine. In 1533, he denounced Clement's authority and married the now-pregnant Anne. That same year, the Archbishop of Canterbury annulled Henry's marriage to Catherine, who died in prayer-filled exile in dark, damp Kimbolton Castle three years later.

Anne Boleyn (c. 1500–36): married 1533; executed 1536. Henry truly loved Anne—just not while they were married. She, too, fell out Henry's favor for not producing a son (their only child would later rule as Queen Elizabeth I). She also had a knack for making enemies among powerful members of Henry's court. Those same enemies, taking advantage of Henry's growing infatuation with Anne's lady-in-waiting, Jane Seymour, pinned trumped-up charges of adultery, witchcraft, and treason on Anne that cost her her head in 1536.

Jane Seymour (1509–37): married 1536, died 1537. Only days after Anne's head rolled, Henry rolled the matrimonial dice with Jane Seymour. Jane produced the male heir Henry longed for (the future Edward VI) in

October 1537 but died of complications from childbirth two weeks later. Her reward was to be the only one of Henry's wives to be buried with him in his Windsor Castle tomb.

Anne of Cleves (1515–57): married January 1540, divorced July 1540. Henry agreed to marry Anne of Cleves with the intention of gaining her brother, the Duke of Cleves, as an ally against France. Upon first glance of Anne, Henry called her a "Flanders mare" and declared his dislike. He married her anyway in January 1540, but his gaze quickly turned to the younger and prettier Catherine Howard. Anne, looking to save her neck, agreed to an annulment seven months later. The man who arranged the marriage, Henry's chief minister, Thomas Cromwell, was beheaded shortly after.

Catherine Howard (c. 1522–42): married 1540, executed 1542. Henry fell hard for Catherine Howard, whom he married 19 days after his annulment from Anne of Cleves. But the 49-year-old Henry lacked the sexual oomph to satisfy teenage Catherine, who began to seek satisfaction from men her age. The jilted Henry had her beheaded for adultery in February 1542.

Katherine Parr (1512–48): married 1543, widowed 1547. Henry took his final marital plunge with the twice-widowed Katherine Parr. Their marriage nearly ended over religious differences, but after patching things up they got along swimmingly—until Henry died in 1547 and made Katherine a widow for a third time.

The Ingredients of Love Potion No. 9

Love potions have long been credited with having major magical influences over the whims and woes of human attraction. Do they work? Well, in the second century AD, Roman writer and philosopher Apuleius allegedly concocted a potion that snagged him a rather wealthy widow. Relatives of the widow even brought Apuleius to court, claiming the witchy potion had worked to subvert the woman's true wishes. Apuleius argued that the potion (supposedly made with shellfish, lobsters, spiced oysters, and cuttlefish) had restored his wife's vivacity and spirit—and the court ended up ruling in his favor.

Yes, love potions have been the stuff of history and legend since ancient times. These alluring elixirs played a major role in Greek and Egyptian mythology, and even made an appearance in the 2004 fairy-tale flick *Shrek 2*. In the movie, the Fairy Godmother gives the King of Far Far Away a bottled potion that is intended to make Fiona fall in love with the first man she kisses.

Turpentine and Indian Ink?

The bottle from *Shrek 2* was marked with a Roman numeral IX, by the way, a clear nod to the formula first made famous in the doo-wop ditty "Love Potion No. 9," which was recorded by The Clovers in 1959 and The Searchers in 1963. According to the song, as penned by legendary songwriters Jerry Leiber and Mike Stoller, the ingredients for the concoction "smelled like turpentine, and looked like Indian ink." Doesn't sound too appealing, huh? Well, it apparently did enough to help a guy who was "a flop with chicks." That is, until he "kissed a cop down on 34th and Vine."

At any rate, if you're a forlorn lover looking to make a little magic of your own, you just might be in luck. In the mid-1990s, Leiber and Stoller worked with former guitarist and part-time perfumer Mara Fox to develop a trademarked cologne spray bearing the name of their hit song.

According to the label, Love Potion #9 is made with water, SD40B alcohol, isopropyl myristate, isopropyl alcohol, and the fragrances of citrus and musk. Can this cool, clean scent really heighten your passion and arousal and make you attractive to the opposite sex? Maybe. But the perfume does come with a disclaimer: "No guarantee of success is granted or implied."

Weird Ways to Attract True Love

It's likely that you or one of your single friends spends a good deal of time complaining about how difficult it is to meet people worth dating. Problem solved! These strange customs from all over the world give single people inventive ways to find true love. Go get an apple and we'll show you.

An Apple a Day . . .

In Elizabethan times, it was desirable for a girl to peel an apple and stick it under her armpit until it was saturated with sweat. The girl would then give it to her potential beau so that he could inhale her heavenly scent. We figure most men would prefer a hanky scented with Chanel N°5, but whatever works.

Eat Your Greens

Ladies, a few directions: Go to Ireland. Find a shamrock. Eat said shamrock while thinking of your true love. Wait for the gentleman to arrive, fully in love with you. In certain parts of Ireland, this custom is said to work like a (lucky) charm.

Backyard Safari

It takes a little preplanning, but if you can spare the time on Valentine's Day, go on a little wildlife adventure to determine your future with love and help your selection process. According to old European folktales, the types of animals you see on February 14 foretell the person you'll marry. Squirrels mean you'll find a cheapskate; goldfinch sightings point to a millionaire; a robin means you'll marry a crime fighter. And if you should find a glove that day, the owner of the other glove is your true love.

Pillaging, Etc.

If you're a warrior or male tribal member who happens to be looking for love, why not try the ancient custom of a hostile takeover? They're always dramatic and you don't have to worry about a curfew. But beware: If your new bride's family comes looking for her, you have to hide out with her for as long as it takes the moon to go through a full cycle.

Spooning

Dating back to 17th-century Wales, men carved spoons when they had a crush on a woman. Much like the secret codes in flower-giving (i.e., red roses=love, daisies=loyalty, etc.), the spoons were carved with various embellishments that let the girl know the man's intentions. Vines meant that feelings continued to grow, for example, and a circle inside a square signified a desire for children.

Victorian Dating Bureaucracy

If you think the politics of dating are weird today, you don't know how good we have it. In the Victorian age, dating among the elite was more complicated than filing taxes. First of all, nothing happened without a chaperone, and everything usually took place in full view of the entire family/town. Before a man could even speak to a woman, he had to be formally introduced. After that, he gave her his card. If the young lady was interested, he might be able to take her out for a stroll. Many "bodice-ripping" books and films are set in the Victorian era—nothing makes for a good story like repressed erotic love.

Sniffin' for Love

A study at the University of New Mexico found that when some women are ovulating, their sense of smell is seriously elevated, allowing them to evaluate how attracted a man is to them just by sniffing his worn shirts. Ladies, if the guy questions your sniffing, just tell him "it's a pheromone thing."

The Baddest of the Bad Boys

What is it about bad boys that women find so appealing? And what about those infamous guys who, despite their horrible deeds, still seem to attract the ladies? Maybe it's as poet Sylvia Plath once wrote, "Every woman adores a fascist."

Adolf Hitler reportedly had a relationship with his 20-year-old half-niece, Geli Raubal, who eventually shot herself. He went on to have several more girlfriends: Fran Hoffman, Jenny Hang, and Helene Hanfstaengl (who prevented Hitler from killing himself). Of course, the gal who would go down in Hitler history was teenager Eva Braun, whom he met in 1929. She became Frau Hitler on April 29, 1945; less than 24 hours later, however, the couple celebrated their honeymoon with a double suicide as the Allies were coming for them.

Hitler contemporary and cohort Joseph Stalin was married to Ekaterina Svanidze, who passed away. Nadezhda Alliluyeva was wife number two, but she later committed suicide (although some allege Stalin murdered her). It was speculated that Stalin was secretly married a third time to his mistress, Rosa Kaganovich.

Commune leader Charles Manson first moved in with UC Berkeley librarian Mary Brunner. Soon he convinced Brunner to allow more women to move in with them— more than a dozen in all. Later, Manson moved to "Spahn Ranch" with his infamous "Manson family," most of whom were female lovers. The infamous 1969 Tate-LaBianca murders were committed by some of these female followers, under Manson's instruction.

After being convicted of the 1989 murders of their parents, brothers Lyle and Erik Menendez both married pen pals they met while serving life sentences. Although Erik and wife Tammi have been married since 1998, the only contact they have is in the prison's public visiting area.

Some women waste no time: Scott Peterson, convicted in 2005 of murdering his wife and unborn child, had barely been on death row an hour when he got his first proposal.

CHAPTER 10
STRANGELY ENTERTAINING

The Dulcet Tones of David Hasselhoff
From *Baywatch* to the Bandstand

As far as Americans are concerned, David Hasselhoff's presence on the entertainment landscape has been benign, unremarkable, and mediocre. Let's face it—nobody watched *Knight Rider* to see 'Hoff in a leather jacket; it was KITT, the talking car, that got viewers to tune in. And it hardly needs mentioning that it wasn't Hasselhoff's hairy chest people were tuning in to check out in *Baywatch*. It would seem obvious, then, that no one would even think about buying a David Hasselhoff album, even if it were in a dollar bin. Well, it might seem obvious to you, but there are several million people who apparently love the man's music. Over the past two decades, 'Hoff has churned out gold and platinum records at an astonishing rate.

There's No Accounting for Taste

Just who is buying these things? The Germans, that's who. And the Austrians and the Swiss. But mostly the Germans. Hasselhoff's popularity in Germany dates back to the late 1980s. At the time, Hasselhoff was in dire straits—*Knight Rider* had ended its brief run in 1986, and 'Hoff's stock couldn't have been any lower in Hollywood. He went to Europe in an attempt to reinvent himself as a soft-rock musician, in much the same way as marginal major-league baseball players go to Japan in desperate attempts to resurrect their careers.

Hasselhoff's reception as a musician was initially tepid, and his success was confined largely to Eastern Europe. Then came 1989—the year the Berlin Wall came tumbling down.

The end of Soviet influence over East Germany was the most momentous historic event in Germany since World War II. That same year, Hasselhoff released a little album called *Looking for Freedom*. Never heard of it? You would have if you'd been in Berlin during those glorious days of reunification. The title song, a cover of a 1970s German hit, had already achieved modest popularity in Eastern Europe in the days leading up to the fall of the Berlin Wall. But Hasselhoff's status in Germany as an iconic rocker was cemented when he performed the song "Looking for Freedom" from atop the crumbling wall during a concert on New Year's Eve in 1989. The song struck a chord with the euphoric Germans, and the album skyrocketed to number one on the country's charts. It stayed there for an incomprehensible eight weeks and eventually was certified triple platinum.

Hasselhoff's singing career has maintained its momentum in Germany—he's put out several albums that have gone at least gold in that country. But it is his performance of "Looking for Freedom" from atop the Berlin Wall that will always be remembered. Thus, one of the iconic moments in the history of their nation is symbolized for millions of Germans by a man who is best known in America for trotting around in red swim trunks.

Frankenstein's Flattop

Lugosi's Lament

It was late spring of 1931 in Hollywood, and actor Bela Lugosi and Universal Studios had struck box office gold with *Dracula*. The film company, sensing a potential bonanza in horror films, immediately cast their new star in the upcoming *Frankenstein*—but, to Lugosi's dismay, he was to play the role of the monster rather than Dr. Frankenstein. Angrily, he wondered why a star of his caliber should play a grunting creature that "any half-wit extra could play." More problems awaited Lugosi in the form of Universal's chief makeup artist Jack P. Pierce. Mr. Pierce and Lugosi had previously clashed on the set of *Dracula*, when the star refused to alter his appearance with pointed teeth and a beard (as author Bram Stoker had described the character).

For *Frankenstein*, Lugosi reluctantly agreed to apply blue-green greasepaint to his face (an effect that appeared gray when shot in black-and-white film), but that's as far as he would go. He and Pierce continued to clash over the monster's appearance, much to the displeasure of the makeup chief. "Lugosi thought his ideas were better than everybody's," Pierce reported with disdain.

When the film's director, Robert Florey, finally shot 20 minutes of *Frankenstein* test footage in June, costar Edward Van Sloan described Lugosi's appearance as "something out of *Babes in Toyland*," commenting that the broad wig made the star's head look four times its normal size, and that his skin was "polished and claylike." Lugosi—who, during the shooting, had threatened to get a doctor's excuse so he wouldn't have to play the part—was through.

"Enough is enough," said the Hungarian actor. "I was a star in my country and will not be a scarecrow over here!"

A Monster Makeover

After Universal executives screened the test footage, they banished both Lugosi and Florey to a lesser project and appointed Englishman James Whale as the new *Frankenstein* director. On Whale's recommendation, they selected an actor Whale had spotted in the Universal commissary—a fellow named Boris Karloff —to play the monster.

Over the next three weeks, Karloff and Pierce worked for three hours every night to develop the monster's signature appearance. The result, including the now-trademark flat head, was one of the most famous makeup jobs in Hollywood history. The unique noggin was no whim: Pierce had spent months researching surgery, anatomy, and other related fields. As he told *The New York Times*, "My anatomical studies taught me that there are six ways a surgeon can cut the skull in order to take out or put in a brain. I figured Frankenstein, who was a scientist but no practicing surgeon, would take the simplest surgical way. He would cut the top of the skull off straight across like a pot lid, hinge it, pop the brain in and then clamp it on tight. That is the reason I decided to make the Monster's head square and flat."

When released in December 1931, *Frankenstein* became an instant smash, and Karloff's rising star quickly eclipsed that of Lugosi. Throughout Karloff's career, he always knew who (or what) to thank for his golden opportunity: the infamous monster, flat head and all.

Maybe Gilligan Was the Smart One

So if the Professor on *Gilligan's Island* could make a radio out of a coconut, why couldn't he fix a hole in a boat? If you were a parent or a child in the 1960s, you're probably familiar with the conundrum at the center of the show.

Gilligan's Island aired on CBS from 1964 to 1967 (and then ad infinitum on TBS, TNT, Nick at Nite, etc.). It was based on a simple premise: A motley group of people on a "three-hour tour" is shipwrecked on a deserted island. One of these shipwrecked tourists was Roy "the Professor" Hinkley, a man with six college degrees and advanced knowledge of technology, science, and obscure island languages.

Over the course of 98 episodes, the Professor was able to create radios, lie detectors, telescopes, and other gadgets out of little more than a few coconuts and some bamboo. In short, the Professor was the MacGyver of his era.

The Confounded Boat Hole

With all of Hinkley's tech wizardry, the question must be asked: Why couldn't he fix a simple boat? (Fortunately, most of the male viewers were too concerned with staring at Mary Ann and Ginger to think logically.) The answer, of course, was ratings. Though *Gilligan's Island* was never a smash hit, it was popular enough to last several seasons. As anybody can tell you, if the Professor had been able to fix the boat, there would have been no show. As it turns out, the Professor and his friends had to wait more than a decade to be rescued. Since CBS canceled the 1968 season of *Gilligan's Island* at the last minute, the final episode of the 1967 season found the crew still stranded on its island. In 1978, a special made-for-TV movie, titled *Rescue from Gilligan's Island*, detailed the crew's long-awaited rescue. It is only fitting that even after a decade, the Professor wasn't able to figure out simple boat repair. Instead, the castaways tied their huts together to make a raft, and floated to freedom, where presumably they spent the rest of their lives watching reruns of themselves on cable television.

Uncovering the Truth about Superheroes

Ever wonder why guys like Superman prance around in a cape and tights? Sure, it seems like an embarrassing outfit, but if it compels criminals to laugh themselves to death, that's good, right?

Cartoonists borrowed the standard superhero outfit—colored tights, trunks, boots, and a cape—from circus strongmen and professional wrestlers of the early 20th century. The outfits certainly made sense at the time. Performers needed tight clothing for maximum flexibility and to give audiences a good look at their muscles. However, lycra and elastic had not been invented; with so much squatting and stretching, performers ran the risk of splitting their tights and exposing their . . . uh . . . little strongmen. So the thinking performer wore trunks over the tights to keep things family-friendly. And since this was show business, flashy colors were essential. This ensemble also worked in early comic books. The illustrator had to show off the hero's muscles, but the character couldn't be running around shirtless—it wasn't proper. A skintight outfit delivered the goods without being offensive. And with some unique colors and a chest emblem, the hero was instantly recognizable.

For flying heroes such as Superman, a cape flapping in the wind, provided a perfect vehicle for illustrating both speed and direction. And, of course, capes were quite in fashion back in the day on the planet Krypton.

The True Story of the World's Favorite Rodent

Walt Disney long held that the inspiration for his most famous creation sprang from a cute little field mouse that visited him at his drawing board in his Kansas City studio. The real story is far more interesting.

In truth, Mickey Mouse was born from a bad business deal. Walt Disney had originally pinned his cinematic success on an animated rabbit named Oswald, only to have the rights to the character stolen from him by New York film distributor Charles Mintz. Desperate for another moneymaking character, Disney brainstormed with his brother, Roy, and lead animator Ub Iwerks.

Various animals were proposed and rejected until the trio finally settled on a mouse—basically because the only other cartoon mouse at the time was George Herriman's Ignatz, of "Krazy Kat" fame. Disney originally wanted to call his new creation Mortimer, but on the advice of his wife, Lilly, he changed it to Mickey.

Mickey's first cartoon was a silent effort titled "Plane Crazy," inspired by Charles Lindbergh's 1927 transatlantic flight. It was quickly followed by "The Gallopin' Gaucho," also a silent cartoon. Distributors were unenthusiastic, so Disney decided to make one more cartoon, this time with synchronized music and sound effects. It was a huge gamble—if the third cartoon failed, Disney would lose everything he had worked so hard to build. "Steamboat Willie" premiered at New York's Colony Theater on November 18, 1928. It was an immediate hit and inspired Disney to add music and sound effects to "Plane Crazy" and "The Gallopin' Gaucho," so the three shorts could be sold to theaters as a package. More cartoons followed, and in just a few years, Disney headed one of Hollywood's most successful and groundbreaking movie studios—thanks to a mouse almost named Mortimer.

Tales from the Orchestra Pit

The Tragedy of Jean-Baptiste Lully

A 17th-century composer named Jean-Baptiste Lully was conducting at a rehearsal, keeping time as usual with a huge wooden staff that he pounded on the floor. One fateful day, however, Lully missed the floor and drove the staff right into his foot. No, this is not the moment the conductor's baton was conceived. Lully did not have an epiphany and say, "You know, I should use something smaller to direct my music." Nevertheless, the moment remains part of music history. An abscess developed on Lully's right foot that turned to gangrene. The composer did not have the foot amputated, causing the gangrene to spread and eventually leading to his death. And there you have it—a conducting fatality!

The Birth of the Baton

So when did conductors trade in those clumsy, and potentially lethal, wooden staves for the symbolically powerful batons? And do they really need them? Don't their hands have ten batons?

Some conductors today use their hands and fingers, but most have a baton that they move to guide the music's tempo. The theory is that the baton—usually 10 to 24 inches long and made of wood, fiberglass, or carbon—magnifies a conductor's patterns and gestures, making them clearer for the orchestra or ensemble.

Orchestras date to the late 16th century during the Baroque period, and conductors back then used the same type of staff that felled Lully. Sometimes there was no conductor at all. Instead, the leader was most often a keyboardist, who would guide the orchestra when his hands were free, or a violinist, who would set the tempo and give directions by beating the neck of his instrument or making other movements. At other times, the keyboardist or violinist simply played louder so the rest of the orchestra could follow his lead. As written music grew more complex, orchestras needed more direction than a keyboardist or violinist could provide. Conductors started appearing in France in the 18th century and emerged in earnest early in the 19th century. Still, there was no baton—rolled up paper was the tool of choice. German composer, violinist, and conductor Louis Spohr claimed to have introduced the formal baton to the music world in a performance in 1820, but he may simply have been boasting. It is widely thought that he only used a baton in rehearsals. Felix Mendelssohn, the German composer, pianist, and conductor, may have been the first to use a real baton in a performance. According to *The Cambridge Companion to Conducting*, Mendelssohn used a baton in 1829 and again in 1832 with the Philharmonic Society of London. The next year, a baton was used regularly with the Philharmonic—and today, almost every conductor wields one.

Baton Wackiness

Even though the baton is a lot safer than the wooden staff, there have been some accidents. For example, German conductor Daniel Turk's motions became so animated during a performance in 1810 that he hit a chandelier above his head and was showered with glass. What is it with these guys?

There was more baton craziness in 2006 and 2007. First, the conductor of the Harvard University band set a record by using a baton that was 10.5 or 12.5 feet long, depending on whom you listen to. The next year, the University of Pennsylvania band claimed to have bested that record with its 15-foot, 9-inch baton. There were no reports of a Lully moment on either occasion.

Where *Is* That Confounded Mule?

Before entering the strange new world of video games in the late 1970s, Nintendo was a small but established Japanese toy company that specialized in producing playing cards. Early in its video game venture, the company found itself stuck with about two thousand arcade cabinets for an unpopular game called *Radar Scope*. Nintendo's president tapped a young staff artist named Shigeru Miyamoto to create a new game that enabled the company to reuse the cabinets.

Miyamato developed an action game in which the player was a little jumping construction worker (named Jumpman, naturally) who had to rescue his lady friend from a barrel-chucking ape. Thanks to the classic movie monster, nothing says "rampaging gorilla" like "Kong," in either English or Japanese, so that part of the name was a no-brainer.

Miyamoto also wanted to include a word that suggested "stubborn" in the title, so he turned to his Japanese-to-English dictionary, which listed "donkey" as a synonym. (English speakers at Nintendo did point out that "Donkey Kong" didn't mean what Miyamoto thought it did, but the name stuck anyway.)

Silly as the name was, things worked out quite well for everyone involved. *Donkey Kong* hit arcades in 1981 and became one of the most successful games in the world, defining Nintendo as a premier video game company in the process. Jumpman changed his name to Mario, became a plumber, and grew into the most famous video game character ever. Miyamoto established himself as the Steven Spielberg of game designers, racking up hit after hit. Sadly, there has yet to be a hit game starring a donkey. Maybe someday Miyamoto will get around to designing one.

Crazy Entertainment Acts

From Vaudeville of old to today's Cirque du Soleil, wacky entertainers have always tried to rule the showman's roost. Here are a few acts that fall outside the traditional entertainment genre but astound, confound, and mesmerize just the same.

Beautiful Jim Key

Starting in the late 1800s, Doc Key and his horse "Beautiful Jim Key" made a mighty strong case for the infinite power of kindness. From 1897 to 1906, the pair thrilled audiences with Jim's uncanny humanlike abilities. Billed as the "Marvel of the Twentieth Century" and "The Greatest Crowd Drawer in America," Jim could read, write, sort mail, tell time, use a cash register and a telephone, and perform a host of other humanlike tasks. But it wasn't always so. In 1889, Jim Key was a sickly, near-lame colt that owner Doc Key half-expected to die. Nurtured by medicines of Doc Key's own concoction, as well as an abundance of love, the little misfit colt was eventually transformed into a gorgeous mahogany bay. People were so taken by Jim Key's abilities that they joined the Jim Key Band of Mercy to the tune of two million members. Their peaceful pledge? "I promise always to be kind to animals."

Growing Man

Billed as "the man who grows before your eyes," Clarence E. Willard could control his muscular and skeletal systems with such astounding ease that he could voluntarily lengthen and shorten his frame by some six inches. From the 1930s through the 1950s, Willard's ability confounded the scientific community as well as his audiences as he stretched from 5'10" to 6'4".

Signora Jo Girardelli

Known as the "incombustible lady," Signora Girardelli had a way with fire. Born in Italy around 1780, the fire-eater distinguished herself by performing daring feats above and beyond those of more pedestrian acts.

She went to great lengths to prove that she was actually *eating*, or defying, fire. Her mediums consisted of nitric acid, molten metal, boiling oil, melted wax, and lit candles. In a performance designed to prove her mettle, Girardelli would fill a pan with boiling oil, drop the white of an egg into it so all could see it cook, fill her mouth with the burning liquid, swish it about for a few seconds for added effect, then spit it out into a brazier where it would instantly blaze up, proving that it was indeed hot oil.

Another favorite bit found Girardelli flaunting her prowess with hot metal. This feat involved heating a shovel until it was red hot and then setting wood ablaze with it. With this accomplished, the performer would stroke her arms, feet, and hair with the burning-hot shovel. No smoke or scorching of any kind was detectable by the audience. At this point, Girardelli was just getting warmed up (pun absolutely intended). The real showstopper arrived seconds later when she *licked* the shovel and an audible hiss was heard from her tongue.

Enrico Caruso: The Superstitious Songster

Details of Caruso's birth in Naples on February 25, 1873, vary widely, but sources say he was the 18th of 21 children in a family that included 19 brothers and a lone sister; most of his siblings died in infancy. Because his mother was too ill, Enrico was nursed by Signora Rosa Baretti. He believed her milk caused him to be different from the rest of his family.

The Caruso family was quite poor—Enrico's father was a mechanic and he encouraged his son to become one as well. Instead, Enrico began singing in churches and cafes at age 16 to help support himself and his family. It may have been his impoverished youth or his need for order that led to his habit of obsessively recording even the most minor purchases in carefully tended books. And yet Caruso was extremely generous, dispensing handouts to almost every-one who asked.

Caruso relocated to the United States after making a big splash at New York's Metropolitan Opera in *Rigoletto* in 1903. Later, while touring with the Met, he found himself smack in the middle of the big 1906 San Francisco earth-quake. Although he escaped unscathed, the experience compelled him to vow never to return. Upon his depar-ture from the city, he is famously known to have shouted, "Give me Vesuvius!" (the explosive volcano of his native Italy that had erupted two weeks earlier).

The Weird Tenor's Tenets

Caruso regulated his life with a rigid set of curious and unexplained superstitions. In her account of Caruso's life, his wife, Dorothy Park Benjamin, revealed that he considered it bad luck to wear a new suit on a Friday, and he shunned the phrase, "Good luck!" for fear it would produce the opposite effect. For reasons unknown, he also refused to start any new undertakings on either a Tuesday or a Friday. Like many artistic geniuses, he was deathly afraid of germs and bathed twice daily, often changing all of his clothes many times a day. As might be expected, some of Caruso's strongest and most peculiar beliefs were related to his magnificent voice. Before going on stage, he performed the following ritual:

1. Smoked a cigarette in a holder so as not to dirty his hands

2. Gargled with salt water to clean his throat

3. Sniffed a small amount of snuff

4. Sipped a cup of water

5. Ate precisely one quarter of an apple

6. Asked his deceased mother to help him sing

Caruso also believed he could enhance his vocal prowess by wearing anchovies around his neck and smoking two packs of cigarettes a day.

The Final Crazy Curtain

Enrico Caruso died in 1921 from complications of bronchial pneumonia. After his death, the Naples Museum in Italy claimed he had left them his throat for examination, and newspapers in Rome printed a diagram of what was supposedly the singer's internal sound system. According to *The New York Times*, doctors said Caruso had vocal cords twice as long as normal, a supersized epiglottis, and the lung power of a "superman." But the *Times* also printed his wife's denial that any organs had been removed from her husband.

Caruso left an almost superhuman legacy of music. With nearly 500 recordings, he remains one of the top-selling artists of record company RCA more than 80 years after his death.

The Great Piano Con

Joyce Hatto was known as an extraordinary pianist. Her recorded repertoire available in the UK grew to more than 100 CDs and included some of the most difficult piano pieces around. What was truly amazing is that she somehow managed to record this music while suffering the effects of cancer and dealing with the usual wear and tear of an aging body. How did she do it? Perhaps her penchant for plagiarism helped. As it turned out, the majority of her works were stolen from other artists' recordings and then reproduced as her own!

Having enjoyed a full, albeit rather insignificant, career as a concert pianist, Hatto abandoned her stage show in 1976 to focus on her advancing disease. On the cusp of 50, she had only a few recorded numbers under her belt. However, that soon changed, as she spent her remaining years prolifically, but as it turned out, falsely, adding to that collection.

The CD Deluge Begins

That Hatto's husband, William Barrington-Coupe, ran the Concert Artists Recordings label under which her recordings were released undoubtedly helped to assist in the harmonious heist. His music-business acumen provided both the technological savvy to engineer the pieces that had been previously released by other pianists and the means to unleash the forged works on an unsuspecting public.

Of course, the scam couldn't last forever. Internet rumors began surfacing in 2005, but *Gramophone*, a monthly music magazine in London, wasn't able to definitively break the news of the deception until February 2007, about eight months after Hatto's death. In fact, her death at age 77 may have actually been an impetus for the discovery.

After Hatto's passing, her celebrity fire burned hotter than ever. Beloved by a small fan base during her life, Hattomania came out in full force upon her death. Some even deemed her one of the great pianists of modern times. But with that superstar status came a renewed flurry of suspicions surrounding the likelihood that a woman of her age and ailing health could produce such a copious collection. *Gramophone* issued a summons for anyone who knew of any fraudulence. Months passed with no evidence. Finally, a reader's computer discovered the deceit, and he contacted the magazine.

The Con Revealed

The reader told the magazine that when he was playing a CD of Hatto hits, his computer identified a particular piece as being performed by little-known pianist Lazlo Simon. *Gramophone* sent the recordings to a sound engineer, who compared sound waves from Hatto's ostensible recording of Liszt's 12 Transcendental Studies to Simon's version. An identical match was uncovered! After that, more and more of the pieces attributed to Hatto were found to belong to other musicians. Hatto and husband had used music technology to recycle other artists' recordings, and that same technology uncovered the deception.

How could they not foresee that music science would reveal them, even as they used its wizardry themselves? Barrington-Coupe has not yet produced a viable answer. Barrington-Coupe eventually confessed to the fraud, insisting that Hatto knew nothing of the scheme and that he had made very little money on it. He claimed that the whole plot was inspired by nothing more than love for his ailing wife and his desire to make her feel appreciated by the music community during her final years. This assertion can neither be proved nor disproved, but *Gramophone* pointed out that Barrington-Coupe continued to sell the false CDs after she died.

CHAPTER 11

AROUND THE WORLD

The People at the Ends of the Earth

Who are these exotic folks? No one, really. They're simply a figure of speech.

Throughout history, people from every culture and walk of life have conjured images of far-off, mythical places with exotic names like Xanadu, Shangri-La, and Milwaukee. This universal desire to fantasize about unknown lands likely gave rise to such terms as "the four corners of the earth" and "the ends of the earth." These phrases suggest that somewhere on our plane of existence exist identifiable, ultimate nether regions—locations farther away from us than any other. A search of the King James Bible turns up no fewer than 28 occurrences of the term "ends of the earth." Psalm 72:8, for example, reads, "He shall have dominion also from sea to sea, and from the river unto the ends of the earth." This is a translation of the Latin *Et dominabitur a mari usque ad mare, et a flumine usque ad terminos terrae.* At a time when guys in togas and sandals went around speaking to each other in Latin, most folks probably did believe that the earth was flat and really did have ends.

Today, most of us don't use the term so literally. It's relative and open to your imagination. The ends of the earth could mean the North Pole. If you live in Paris or Rome, perhaps it means the remote Amazon jungle. And if you live on a Himalayan peak, maybe it means Milwaukee.

Why Aren't There Southern Lights?

There are. The southern lights are called the "aurora australis," and according to those who've seen them (including famed explorer Captain James Cook, who named the lights in 1773), they are just as bright and alluring as the aurora borealis in the north. We don't hear about them because the viewing area—around the geomagnetic South Pole—is mostly unpopulated.

Northern or southern, the lights are the result of solar storms that emit high-energy particles. These particles travel from the sun as a solar wind until they encounter and interact with the earth's magnetic field. They then energize oxygen atoms in the upper atmosphere, causing light emissions that can appear to us as an arc, a curtain, or a green glow. If these oxygen atoms get really excited, they turn red.

There are other atoms in the ionosphere, and they produce different colors when they're titillated by those solar winds. Neutral nitrogen will produce pink lights, and nitrogen radicals glow blue and violet.

Usually, the lights are visible only in latitudes between ninety degrees (at the poles) and thirty degrees. In the north, that large swath includes most of Europe, Asia (excluding India, except for its northernmost tip, and southern countries such as Myanmar, Thailand, and Cambodia), the United States, and Canada. In the south, though, only the southernmost tips of Australia and Africa and the countries of Chile, Argentina, and Uruguay in South America are within that zone.

So in reality the question is this: If a light shines in the south and there is no one there to see it, does it still dazzle?

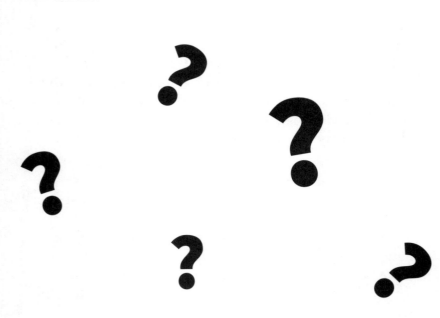

Here Comes Papai Noel

. . . with a suntan! Brazilians don't associate Christmas with snow and "Jack Frost nipping at your nose." That's because it's summer in the South American country, and even Papai Noel (the Brazilian version of Santa Claus, imported from North America in the 1950s) has to dress in a lightweight silk suit to keep cool. Some people celebrate the holiday by hitting the beach and watching fireworks or having a BBQ.

Leave That Baby Alone!

Since Brazil was once a colony of Portugal, many Christmas traditions in the country are of Portuguese origin, including the popular *presépio* or nativity scene. Derived from the word "presepium" (meaning a bed of straw

where the Christ child lay), elaborate presépio pop up
in many places throughout the Christmas season. Some
Brazilians enact the traditional play *Los Pastores* ("The
Shepherds"), which is also performed in Mexico—except
Brazil's version features shepherdesses instead of shep-
herds and a gypsy who sneaks in and tries to snatch baby
Jesus from his straw bed!

Who am I?

Christmas decorations include giant illuminated trees
and fresh flowers. Many Brazilians celebrate the holiday
by exchanging clues with an *amigo secreto* (a "Secret
Santa" of sorts) whose identity is not revealed until
Christmas, accompanied by the giving of a special gift.

Up until that point, participants conceal their identity by corresponding with fake names (or *apelidos*).

The Christmas meal is often a lavish affair, featuring roast turkey and ham, seasonal fruits and vegetables, beans, and rice. Some families attend mass on December 24 and then eat their special dinner at midnight. Others attend midnight mass or *Missa do Galo* (*galo* meaning "rooster," since the service traditionally ends at 1 a.m.), although this mass is no longer as widely observed. As is the tradition in many countries, on Christmas morning, children open presents that were delivered in the night by Papai Noel.

Twelve Countries with the Highest Beer Consumption

COUNTRY	GALLONS PER PERSON
1. Ireland	41.0
2. Germany	32.0
3. Austria	28.0
4. Belgium (tied)	26.0
5. Denmark (tied)	26.0
6. United Kingdom	25.5
7. Australia	23.5
8. United States	22.4
9. Netherlands (tied)	21.0
10. Finland (tied)	21.0
11. New Zealand	20.5
12. Canada	18.5

Luck of the Irish

Yes, it's true: There are no snakes in Ireland, and there never have been.

Snakes have never set foot, er, slithered into Ireland, so there's no validity to the rumor that Saint Patrick rid the country of the scaly reptiles by driving them into a sea of green beer. Just kidding . . . about the beer, not the snakes.

Initially, what is now known as Ireland lacked a climate that was warm enough to accommodate snakes. About 8,500 years ago, temperatures rose enough to make Ireland a nice home for slitherers, but it wasn't to be. The veritable heat wave melted the ice that connected Ireland to Europe, and it became the island that it is today. Talk about the luck of the Irish: Since it was surrounded by water, it was beyond the reach of those scary snakes.

So why does Great Britain, Ireland's closest neighbor and also an island, have snakes? Great Britain was connected to Europe until about 6,500 years ago. Three species of snakes made it to Great Britain before the melting glaciers created the English Channel and isolated it from the mainland. Great Britain is as far as the snakes got— by then, Ireland was an island.

In addition to lacking snakes, Ireland has only one species of lizard, frog, toad, and newt. In the 1960s, humans introduced the "slow worm," a legless lizard that some mistake for a snake, into the wild.

What about the legend of Saint Patrick driving the snakes from Ireland ? Well, as anyone who majored in English in college knows, allegory is a powerful form of storytelling. In the case of Saint Patrick, snakes might have represented pagans as he worked tirelessly to convert people to Christianity.

If you really hate snakes, you'll be heartened to learn that Ireland isn't the only place on the planet without them. New Zealand, Iceland, Greenland, and Antarctica are also snake-free.

Werewolves of Germany

Werewolf sightings may be the least reported sightings out of all the paranormal experiences one can stumble upon. Maybe it's not too often that you find yourself alone at night in the German or English countryside during a full moon; or maybe you do and you've just gotten lucky so far. German towns have been plagued with folklore of werewolves for a long time, and in 1988, one report of the infamous Morbach Monster had locals in a panic when their safeguard failed them.

The folklore around the Morbach Monster dates back to the early 19th century when a fighter in Napoleon's army deserted the war effort with a group of Russians near the village of Wittlich, Germany. During his sojourn in the German countryside away from battle, Thomas Johannes Baptist Schwytzer attacked and killed a local farmer and his wife. But, rumors say the wife was able to curse the man before she was killed.

What was the curse, you ask? Well, purportedly the woman cursed the man to wander full-mooned nights as a beast, terrifying and killing anyone who was unlucky enough to cross paths with it. The story goes that the villagers set out one full moon, fed up with the terror, to hunt, capture, and destroy the beast before it destroyed them. The hunt was a success. They put an end to the beast's reign of terror. But they could not guarantee that it wouldn't come back, so they created a shrine in which to burn candles during a full moon, thwarting the beast from entering the town.

Nearly two hundred years later, the candle still burned through the evenings every twenty-nine days. A full-mooned night in 1988 saw this safeguard fail, scaring the ranks of U.S. military men occupying a base nearby. The soldiers had all heard the local rumors of werewolves and knew about the shrine that kept them away, but as they passed the shrine that night they noticed the candle had gone out. Not taking any of the local lore seriously, they joked about how the werewolf would inevitably be seen that night.

Later that night, the Morbach U.S. Air Force Base was awoken to sirens signaling that the perimeter of the base had been breached. One soldier who kept guard said he saw a large beast trying to get past the gates, but it then ran back into the forest as the spotlight was shone upon it.

In an uproar, the men went searching for the monster. Search dogs had their nose to the ground and obviously had a scent to follow, but at a certain point, the dogs would lead no further. The dogs seemed reluctant to continue the hunt, which obviously also took the fire out of the soldiers' motivation as well. The men turned back to the base that night with their eyes watching behind them, filled with a new respect for German folklore.

What was it that they tried to find that night? Was it really the Morbach Monster coming back after nearly two hundred years to feast on the villagers and U.S. military men? Or was it just a tale believed a little too much by the locals?

"Siberia" for Siberians

The frozen and desolate expanse of Siberia is infamous as a place of forced exile for Russian political dissidents. But if you already lived in Siberia and ran afoul of the authorities, where would you be sent?

If you lived in Siberia and were exiled, you'd probably wind up in a prison elsewhere in Russia—and anywhere would likely be better than Siberia. Russia is the world's largest country by landmass, and Siberia accounts for more than 75 percent of it—it's about 5.2 million square miles. Until very recently, large areas of Siberia were difficult to get to . . . and, thus, difficult to escape from. This made it an ideal place to send those who questioned Russian authority. The Russian government started banishing people to distant parts of the country—not just Siberia—around the 17th century, and it continued to do so until after World War II.

Political and criminal exiles were sent to Siberian labor camps known as gulags. Many of these gulags were in remote areas in northeast Siberia. Sevvostlag, a system of labor camps, was set up in the Kolyma region, within the Arctic Circle. Parts of the Kolyma mountain range weren't even discovered until 1926. It's a land of permafrost and tundra, with six-month-long winters during which the average temperature range is –2 degrees to –36 degrees Fahrenheit.

Siberia's first settlements were established relatively late in Russia's history, around the 17th century, but the region now supports several cities of more than half a million people. These are situated mostly in the south and have been accessible by rail since the early 20th century. The storied Trans-Siberian Railway runs from Moscow east to Vladivostok, a distance of about 5,800 miles. The workforce that built the railway consisted of soldiers and, yes, labor-camp inmates.

Confederate Rebels
South of the Equator

Confederados they call them in Brazil: post-Civil War Southerners who fled to the tropics. In the southern Brazilian state of São Paulo, there survives a town named Americana where the great-great-grandchildren of Confederate rebels speak in a Georgia drawl with a Portuguese accent. They are descendants of the Confederados, a group of Southerners who settled in Brazil after the Civil War ended. Every year, a diminishing number of offspring reunite for the *Festa Confederada*, a celebration of Dixie culture. They serve deep-fried chicken, fly the Confederate flag, dress in antebellum fashion, and downplay the issue of slavery.

Fleeing the South

In the post-Civil War upheaval, a Confederate migration found tens of thousands of people escaping to Europe, Mexico, and beyond. While the 2,500 who settled in Mexico ultimately saw their hopes dashed and were forced to return to the United States, the 9,000 who continued "way, way down South" to Brazil found a dependable protector in its emperor, Dom Pedro II. He wanted the Southerners to bring state-of-the-art cotton-farming know-how to his country.

Pedro was gradually phasing out slavery in Brazil. His daughter, Princess Isabel, would end the institution with the stroke of a pen, ushering in the Golden Law of abolition in 1888. But with a few exceptions, the Confederados didn't appear to have brought all the practices of their antebellum plantations to the tropics. A recent study by Brazilian researcher Alcides Gussi was able to find evidence of only 66 slaves owned by four families of Confederados in Brazil. Many of the immigrants were too poor to own slaves, and the rest relied largely on cheap local labor.

A New Home

By the end of the 1860s, Southerners were steaming for Brazil from the ports of New Orleans, Charleston, Newport News, Baltimore, and Galveston to settle in towns such as Americana and nearby Santa Bárbara D'Oeste. "My grandfather came from Texas and built his house in the middle of a forest," 86-year-old Maria Weissinger told the *Atlanta Journal-Constitution* in 2003. The new land was fertile but rife with insects that carried deadly tropical diseases. Many refugees gave up and returned to the Reconstruction South, but about two in five stayed in their adopted homeland, intermarried with Brazilians, grew pecans and peaches, and built schools and universities.

Weakened Roots

After nearly 150 years, most of the Confederados have been absorbed into the populations of big cities, but in the industrial town of Americana, traces of the South survive, kept alive in part by a group called the Fraternity of American Descendants. Multiple generations in, the lines between Confederados and Brazilians have become more blurred than ever. Many of the observant Confederados in Americana no longer speak English, but many continue to travel to a cemetery in nearby Santa Bárbara D'Oeste, where the graves tell the stories of their families' fading Confederate roots. In 1972, the cemetery was visited by one settler's great-niece: Rosalyn Carter, wife of future president Jimmy Carter, then governor of Georgia.

The Most Crowded Place on Earth

We know what you're thinking: The most crowded place on Earth must be Disneyland on the first day of summer vacation, or perhaps the Mall of America on the morning after Thanksgiving. Right? Wrong.

Packed In Like Sardines

While places like Disneyland and the Mall of America are definitely hectic at certain times, there is a section of Hong Kong that has them both beat 365 days a year. It's called Mong Kok, which translates to "flourishing/busy corner." The name is apt because, according to *Guinness World Records*, Mong Kok is the most densely populated place on the planet.

About 200,000 people reside in Mong Kok, an area just slightly larger than half a square mile. That's about 70 square feet per person. Add in the buildings and you've got a district in which it is physically impossible for everyone to be outside at the same time. Mong Kok's bustling Golden Mile—a popular stretch of shops, restaurants, and theaters—compounds the crowding issue: A half-million or so tourists routinely jostle for position in the streets. Residents told *The New York Times* that the streets are often completely full, with every inch of pavement covered.

Going Up, Up, Up

How is it possible to squeeze so many people into such a small area? You build up. Mong Kok is home to an array of high-rise apartment buildings. Families who live in these apartments sometimes rent out rooms to other families. There might be ten or more people in a single apartment—they sleep in two or three rooms and share a small kitchen and a single bathroom. The apartments are so small that people sleep in bunk beds that are three or four tiers high, and they keep their belongings in chests and baskets that are suspended from the ceiling.

Remember Mong Kok the next time you're elbowing your way through a crowded store on Black Friday, trying to secure the season's must-have toy. When you return home and sit at the table for dinner, at least there won't be two other families smiling back at you.

Have You Lost Weight?
The Great Canadian Gravity Dip

Ah, gravity. It keeps our feet—and everything else—firmly on the ground. But due to some (literally) heavy geological history, in some parts of Canada, gravity is a matter of opinion.

Ice, Ice Baby

If you had been hanging out in North America 20,000 years ago, you would have needed to bundle up. At the time, the world was enduring the last major Ice Age, and glaciers covered a sizable chunk of the continent. In some places, the ice sheet was about two miles thick.

As you can imagine, that ice was also pretty heavy. In fact, the ice sheet was so dense that the Earth's crust sagged under its weight until it finally melted away approximately 14,000 years ago. After the big melt, most of the ground popped up to its original shape, but parts of Canada have yet to bounce back.

Up, Up, and Away!

The result of these still-sagging areas of the Earth is what scientists call a "gravity dip." The anomaly seems to be centered around the Hudson River region. These dips occur when parts of the ice-squashed earth get stuck in their Ice Age positions. Some people would regard the result as unfair: Most people who step on a scale in that area will weigh less than you, even if pound for pound, the two of you weighed the same. Scientists believe that in addition to the crust-sagging activity that occurred, a layer of lava in the Earth's mantle also plays a role in creating the gravity dips.

Whatever the reason, don't get too excited: A gravity dip doesn't mean that your sandwich is going to float off into space. Most of the benefits are purely scientific. As one researcher said, "We are able to show that the ghost of the ice age still hangs over North America."

World's Oldest Parliament

Contrary to popular belief, the world's oldest parliament is not in Britain. It's not in the United States, either.

First, a Definition

A parliament is a representative assembly with the power to pass legislation and most commonly consists of two chambers, or houses, in which a majority is required to create and amend laws. Congress became the supreme legislative body of the United States in 1789. The roots of the British Parliament date back to the 12th century, but it wasn't until 1689 that the Bill of Rights established Parliament's authority over the British monarch and gave it the responsibility of creating, amending, and repealing laws.

The title of Oldest Functioning Legislature in the World belongs to the Parliament of Iceland, known as *Althing*, which is Icelandic for "general assembly." Althing was established in AD 930 during the Viking age. The legislative assembly met at Thingvellir (about 30 miles outside of what is now the country's capital, Reykjavik) and heralded the start of the Icelandic Commonwealth, which lasted until 1262. Althing convened annually and served as both a court and a legislature. One of Althing's earliest pieces of legislation was to banish the Viking explorer Erik the Red from Iceland in 980 after he was found guilty of murder.

Even after Iceland lost its independence to Norway in 1262, Althing continued to hold sessions, albeit with reduced powers, until it was dissolved in 1799. In 1844, Althing was restored as an advisory body, and in 1874 it became a legislative body again, a function it maintains to this day. The parliament is now located in Reykjavik.

Ten Countries with the Highest Life Expectancy

Want to live to a ripe old age? By far the most important factor in life expectancy is wealth; richer people tend to eat healthfully, smoke and drink less, and have access to the best health care. Affluent countries also tend to have low rates of violent crime and civil unrest. The following countries have the highest average life expectancies in the world. In case you're wondering, the United States, with an average life expectancy of 77.85, ranks 48th.

1. Andorra: 83.51

The tiny country of Andorra is located between France and Spain. It was one of Europe's poorest countries until it became a popular tourist destination after World War II. Its 71,000 inhabitants now enjoy all the benefits of a thriving economy, which include excellent nutrition and public health-care facilities.

2. Macau: 82.19

Like Andorra, this island in the South China Sea is reaping the rewards of a booming economy. The money has come from visitors, particularly from the Chinese mainland, coming to take advantage of a recently liberalized gaming industry. Gambling profits now provide about 70 percent of the country's income, and the government uses the money to invest heavily in public health care.

3. San Marino: 81.71 (tied)

This enclave in central Italy is the third smallest state in Europe (after Vatican City and Monaco), as well as the world's oldest republic. Here, the long life expectancy is due to prosperity and the fact that the majority of the population is involved in office-based work rather than heavy industry and labor, which shorten life spans.

4. Singapore: 81.71 (tied)

Aside from prosperity, one factor in Singapore's long average life expectancy is that in the early 1980s, the government recognized that it had an aging population, with the average age of its citizens increasing all the time. The government planned accordingly, and now Singapore has excellent health-care facilities for the elderly.

5. Hong Kong: 81.59

People in Hong Kong generally eat a healthful and balanced diet, based around rice, vegetables, and tofu, with only small amounts of meat. This means that obesity rates are low, as are the rates for most dietary-based cancers and heart disease.

6. Japan: 81.25

Japan has one of the lowest adult obesity rates in the industrialized world, at only 3 percent. As in Hong Kong, this is mainly due to a healthful diet based around vegetables, fish, rice, and noodles. Many Japanese people also stop eating when they feel about 80 percent full, rather than continuing until they can't manage another mouthful. The Japanese are also much less reliant on cars than people in Western countries, preferring to walk whenever possible, and therefore get plenty of exercise.

7. Sweden: 80.51 (tied)

Although an economic downturn in the late 1990s did some damage to Sweden's world-renowned welfare and public health systems, they are still among the best in the world. Also, Sweden has the lowest rate of smokers in the developed world—about 17 percent—so tobacco-related deaths are half the European average.

8. Switzerland: 80.51 (tied)

Aside from a stable economy with all of the usual factors that increase longevity, such as a healthful diet and high standard of health care, Switzerland's much-vaunted neutrality means that its inhabitants are highly unlikely to die in an armed conflict.

9. Australia: 80.50

All the usual factors relating to prosperity apply here, but the life expectancy of indigenous Australians is about 20 years less than that of white Aussies, due to higher rates of just about every factor that shortens life, including smoking, obesity, and poverty. Incidentally, research suggests that Australia's life expectancy may start falling as obesity reaches epidemic proportions in the land down under.

10. Guernsey: 80.42

The island of Guernsey, located in the English Channel, is a British Crown dependency, but it is not part of the UK. The reason for its high life expectancy is simple: it's extremely wealthy. Very low taxes make Guernsey a popular destination for tax exiles who can afford the very best in nutrition and medical care. More than half of the island's income comes from financial services— which means well-paid desk jobs—with very few people working in heavy industry.

Uncommon Qualities of World Languages

Human language is as diverse as its speakers. Grammar is the brick and mortar of language, and a given language may have grammar elements unique to its linguistic family. Non-native speakers find certain languages particularly tough, and many potential trip-ups are amusing.

* Thanks to centuries of Moorish occupation, Arabic was a major influence on Spanish—*el* (masculine "the") is directly borrowed. So is *ojalá qué* ("would that" or "may it be so"); you can see the name Allah quite easily in that wishing phrase. Students practice it by wishing that Spanish had fewer verb tenses.

* In Hebrew you don't say, "I like it"; you say, "It finds favor in my eyes." When Eliezer ben Yehuda resurrected conversational Hebrew, he used biblical forms to accommodate the needs of 20th-century language. Another was the use of the biblical "Behold . . ." for "Here is/are . . . ." Even the Israeli Defense Forces picked it up, naming one tank Sho't ("scourge" or "lash") and another Merkava ("chariot"). Behold: a challenging but beautiful modern language with firm roots in antiquity!

* Each Chinese character can have several unrelated meanings depending on the pronunciation, based on the tonal (type of intonation, such as rising or falling). This isn't as confusing as it might sound; simply learn the correct tone when you learn the word and repeat it until a native speaker gives you the thumbs-up. If you get it wrong, you could say something amusing and/or embarrassing.

* Visitors to Hungary often get a rude surprise when asking directions to the city of Szeged. It's pronounced "SEGG-ed" in Magyar, but many tourists mistakenly ask the way to "SHEGG-ed," which would actually mean "your rear end." Known for their spirited sense of comedy, Hungarians have been known to answer tourists by turning around and bending over.

* Until the 1970s, there were two official variations of modern Greek: Demotic (popular) and Katharevousa. Demotic Greek is what you speak today when you stop for a friendly chat with Mr. Kypriotakis; Katharevousa was a ceremonial version incorporating classical elements for government and formal usage. Like Sweden, Greece

has the luxury of sole ownership of its national language—thus, Greek is whatever the Greeks say is Greek.

* Some Semitic languages (Hebrew, Arabic, Aramaic) are
written from right to left. Left-handed persons taking up
Semitic language calligraphy make a happy discovery:
There's no need to worry about smearing the ink as
they write.

* Many languages change verbs with suffixes, but Swahili
does this mostly with prefixes to the verb's root. It's not
limited to verbs: Swahili calls itself kiSwahili, ki- being the prefix to denote a language. The people of the
Swahili coast refer to themselves as wa-Swahili. Swahili
is part of the vast Bantu language family of southern
Africa, in which similar prefixing concepts are common.
Now you see why old *National Geographic* magazines
heavy-handedly called the Tutsi "Watusi" (should have
been "waTutsi")—thus burning that name into millions
of teenage brains and inspiring the 1960s dance craze
and the Orlons song.

* Hebrew is gender-intensive; even verbs are conjugated
by gender. In Hebrew dialogue, participants' genders become evident within a few sentences. You have to know
someone's gender to ask how he or she is doing.

* In some Spanish-speaking countries, the verb *coger*
means "to catch" (as in a taxi or bus). In others, it means
to have sex. So in some places, if you ask where you may
coger un autobus, you'll encounter shocked disapproval
at your vulgarity. Less stuffy listeners might be greatly
amused—and even guide you to a bus so they can see
just how this is accomplished!

Touring the Ancient World

Pleasure cruises? Country retreats? Visits to ancient monuments? Tourism didn't just start with the opening of Disneyland. This human peculiarity has roots that trace back to the ancient world.

"On Your Left, the Hanging Gardens . . ."

What did the very earliest tourists enjoy? Cuddly saber-toothed kittens at the petting zoo? Tar-pit paddle boat rides? Well, that was prehistory, and tourism wasn't yet an industry, but with the passing of many centuries, city-states and empires became sophisticated enough that tourism was feasible. Visitors couldn't enjoy Six Flags over Carthage, but that's only because it hadn't been invented. There were other places to go and things to see, but travel beyond one's own borders was nevertheless a risky proposition.

By the first millennium BC, Near Eastern empires had developed waterways, roads, lodging, and systems of commerce sufficient to encourage tourism. Even better, there was a mass of potential tourists to make added investment in infrastructure worthwhile. Then with the rise of the Persian Empire in mid-millennium (around 500 BC), two additional key elements—peace and effective government—made tourism not just possible but relatively pleasant.

The earliest tourist destinations evident in the Western historical record are Babylon (present-day Iraq) and Egypt. Both destinations had neat things to see: the Hanging Gardens, pyramids, temples, festivals, and street markets. The ancient world also had museums, light-houses, religious celebrations, and a lively system of commerce to lure well-heeled visitors.

Going Greek

When Greece caught the attention of curious travelers around 500 BC, visitors favored the sea route rather than brave the wilds of Asia Minor (modern Turkey). At about the same time, the Levantine ports of what are now Syria, Lebanon, and Israel flourished. In the 400s BC, Greeks wrote travel guides that evaluated locations and facilities—a little like *Lonely Planet*, but at that time the known limits of the planet were much smaller.

Greek and Levantine destinations attracted visitors, but tourists still had to remain on guard. In those days, people carried cash (no credit cards, right?), which attracted the attention of swindlers, pickpockets, and cut-throats. Seas around favored ports were controlled well enough to allow local and regional commerce to thrive, but a ship full of people wearing the ancient equivalent of Bermuda shorts was easy prey for pirates. Until things became safer and easier, tourism couldn't grow.

Roamin' Romans

With its seafaring rival Carthage put out of the way by 202 BC, Republican Rome began its rise to undisputed dominance of the Mediterranean Sea. By the time Rome had a bona fide empire (about 27 BC), well-laid Roman roads encircled *Mare Nostrum* ("our sea"), with inns spaced just a day's travel apart. Armed patrols ensured the security of land routes. The Roman fleet aggressively hunted down pirates, making sea travel safer than ever before. Roman maps told travelers where they might go; chroniclers offered details about the sites.

Many would-be travelers had the hardy soul that was required, but then as today, serious travel was for the affluent. Most Romans were too poor to enjoy the diversions of new places. And even for those who could afford visits to Athens, Judea, and Egypt, the land route meant overpriced food of unpredictable quality and uncomfortable lodging. The Mediterranean's sea lanes may have been swept of pirates, but nothing could be done about storms and other nautical hazards. Mindful of this risk, Romans struck bargains with the gods before travel, promising to do this or that in return for a safe voyage. Of course, even the most attentive Roman gods couldn't guarantee a *pleasant* trip.

Fun and Games for Grownups

So what was there to see and do around *Mare Nostrum?* For the simple pleasures of gluttony and sin, one might try the western Italian coast. Although Sparta was some 300 years into decline by AD 1, travelers were drawn there by the echoes of its martial past and by the quaint Spartan notion of equality between the sexes.

Athens had reached its Classical-era peak around the fifth century BC, and was in decline by the first century AD, but was swarmed with visitors drawn by the city's architecture and sculpture. In Egypt, the pyramids remained a major attraction, and Alexandria had the fabulous library that dedicated itself to collecting all of the world's knowledge. Then there was *Novum Ilium* (New Troy), also known as Troy IX, as the site had been destroyed or abandoned, and subsequently rebuilt, many times over the centuries. In 85 BC, the Romans put it back together as a living memorial to their supposed Trojan heritage, with enough Greek and Persian touches tacked on to further intrigue travelers. Other Mediterranean destinations and diversions included zoos, freak shows, prostitutes, exotic foods—and above all, bragging rights for having undertaken a pleasure trip in the first place. The ancient traveler was considered nothing if not cosmopolitan.

Two-way

Because "Rome" signified a still-vast empire by the first century AD, the city not only provided a class of tourists who traveled from the city, but hosted countless citizens who came to Rome from the empire's farther reaches. These visitors were inevitably impressed, and not a little intimidated, by the city's sprawl, grime, and confusion. More than a million people lived in Rome, and the effect of the city upon visitors from quieter realms must have been breathtaking—and not always in a pleasant way. Still, any provincial who returned from *Roma Eterna* was hailed back home as a sophisticate, just as a Roman who could speak gracefully about the ancient route of the Greek poet Homer enjoyed an elevated social status.

As Rome declined, so did tourism, but pleasure travel never died out completely. Although today's Mediterranean tour guides, bus drivers, trinket sellers, and desk clerks may not realize it, they are practitioners of a popular art that is ancient and perhaps even noble.

Survival on the High Seas

Humankind has been subjected to every imaginable hostile condition, but very little beats the grueling stories of survival for days, weeks—even months—lost at sea.

Hold On Tight

Oceangoing tales of survival have a certain mythic status. They bring to mind epic travels; age-old yarns of sea monsters, mermaids; and nourishment via filtered water and the sucked bones of fish. Yet legend aside, even factually verified survival stories seem implausible. To be stranded on the sea (and to live to tell the tale) seems, well, unreal.

A hierarchy applies when gauging the relative extremity of a sea survival story. Those in cold water are the worst off, since hypothermia sets in within minutes. Survival time also depends on whether there's something to hold onto, or the person is simply treading water. Survival time is also cut short by solitude—humans have a difficult time being alone for extended periods. The best-case scenario, if such a scenario exists, is to be stranded on a boat, in warm water, along with some comrades. What follows are some recent record breakers that run the gauntlet of these hapless scenarios:

Juan Jesus Caamano Survived 13 hours with no boat in cold waters

In 2001, a fishing boat capsized off the coast of Spain. Nine of the 16 men made it into a lifeboat, another two jumped into the frigid waters without putting on their bodysuits (and died immediately), while five others managed to get their suits on before the boat sank.

Two of those five were 36-year-old Juan Jesus Caamano and his brother-in-law. Their boat had sent out a mayday signal before sinking, so planes, helicopters, and ships from several countries were sent to look for the victims. After only four hours, the nine men in the lifeboat were saved. Experts, who estimated a man in Caamano's circumstances could survive a maximum of 3 1/2 hours, were surprised when, after 13 hours, Caamano was found alive, afloat in the stormy waters, tied to his dead brother-in-law. In all, six men died.

Laura Isabel Arriola de Guity
Survived six days; found clinging
to driftwood in warm waters

In 1998, Hurricane Mitch devastated the coasts of Central and Latin America, killing more than 7,000 people in Honduras alone. Isabella Arriola, 32, lived in a small coastal Honduran village that was literally swept away by the ocean. She survived for six days with no life jacket, drifting in and out of consciousness, while clinging to pieces of driftwood. Somehow, she survived through high waves and winds that climbed to 185 mph. Arriola was eventually spotted by a coast guard aircraft and was rescued by helicopter. Unfortunately, she found that her husband, children, and half her village had perished in the storm.

Steven Callahan Survived
76 days on a small raft

In 1982, Steven Callahan, a naval architect, was participating in a sailing race when his boat was damaged during a storm and sank in the Atlantic Ocean. Callahan somehow managed to salvage a tiny amount of food from the sinking craft before setting off in an inflatable rubber raft. He survived on the open ocean for 76 days, living on rainwater, fish, and seabirds before being rescued by a fishing boat. Callahan's extensive background and experience with the high seas helped him survive the ordeal. He holds the longest known record for surviving alone on a raft.

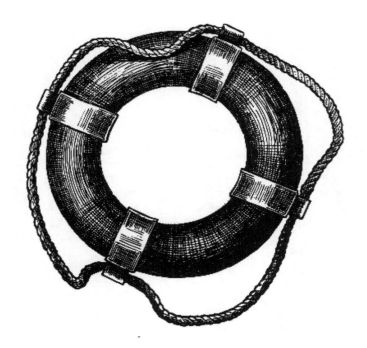

Maralyn and Maurice Bailey
Survived 117 days on a small raft

In 1973, British couple Maralyn and Maurice Bailey set out on an ambitious voyage from England to New Zealand on their yacht, which was struck by a large whale and capsized off the coast of Guatemala. Maurice happened to be an expert on maritime survival skills; before they boarded their rubber raft, they collected a small amount of food, a compass, a map, an oil burner, water containers, and glue. When the Baileys ran out of food, they caught sea animals with safety pins fashioned into hooks. After two months, the raft started to disintegrate, and it needed constant care. Finally, 117 days later, a small Korean fishing boat rescued them.

Crater of Light

On the western edge of the Painted Desert northeast
of Flagstaff, Arizona, a dormant volcano is the setting for
an elaborate art project. Quaker artist James Turrell purchased the 400,000-year-old, two-mile crater in 1979,
and since then he has been carving out tunnels, rooms,
and circular openings that allow in light and a view of
the sky. But when will Roden Crater be completed and
visitors let in? That's a question Turrell fans—and others
who "dig" land art installations—have been asking
for years.

Digging a Hole

Throughout his artistic career, Turrell has played with space, light, and perspective. In fact, some people call him a "sculptor of light." He designed the Live Oak Meeting House in Houston, Texas, for the Society of Friends. It features what he calls a "skyspace," a square in the roof that opens to sky, creating (according to Turrell, speaking on a PBS program) "a light that inhabits space, so that you feel light to be physically present." Skyspaces pop up in other works by Turrell—such as a hotel and art gallery he codesigned on Japan's Benesse Island—and their particular shapes and angles allow light to enter in stunning ways.

Turrell spotted Roden Crater while he was working as an aerial cartographer. At the time, he was interested in land art, and he envisioned a series of tunnels and light-filled chambers inside the volcano. The entire place would function as a kind of naked-eye observatory in which visitors could observe the sun, moon, stars, clouds, and amazing celestial events. With its low light pollution and warm, clear climate, Arizona is perfectly suited to this kind of observation.

Time and Money

Using grants from the prestigious Guggenheim Foundation and the Dia Art Foundation, Turrell purchased the crater and got to work moving tons of earth to fulfill his artistic vision. This has been an architectural project as much as an artistic one. It turns out that moving tons of earth takes a lot of effort . . . and money. But the artist did not want to scale back his plans. When certain funding sources dried up, Turrell had to look elsewhere for help, such as the Macarthur Foundation and the Santa Fe-based Lannan Foundation.

The project was supposed to take a few years but it actually has been ongoing for decades. Still closed to the public, Roden Crater has no official opening date. That said, there are certain completed features, including a long tunnel through the heart of the volcano and a pair of breathtaking skyspaces that frame the Arizona sky above.

According to Turrell, the completed art piece will include more than 1,000 feet of tunnels and seven viewing rooms, as well as a feature called "The Eye of the Crater," situated 38 feet below the volcano's center.

Meanwhile, Turrell's admirers can't wait to see the finished product. Some people have snuck onto the site to see the work-in-progress and snap some pictures. A few art critics and VIPs have been invited inside the crater. Roden Crater was featured on a show in the UK called *Sculpture Diaries* and on the PBS program *Art: 21*. In 2007, it was the subject of a *New York Times* article in which the reporter, Jori Finkel, stressed just how highly anticipated it is: The crater, she said, "is one of the

hottest tickets around. Writers have compared it to Stonehenge and the Mexican pyramids." Others have predicted that the cinder cone will be the "Sistine Chapel" of the United States or one of our newest "Wonders of the World."

Once open, no doubt Roden Crater will be recognized as something spectacular—a blend of art and architecture that, by placing light at the center, will seem effortless in its construction, even though it took years to complete.

CHAPTER 12

INFAMOUS FOOTNOTES TO THE FAMOUS

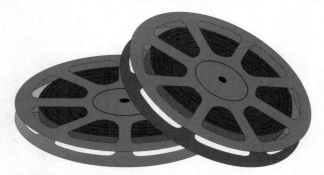

Errol Flynn and the Cuban Rebel Girls

The final screen appearance of virile Hollywood leading man Errol Flynn is a shocker. It seems inconceivable that the man who had starred in *The Adventures of Robin Hood* and *The Sea Hawk* should place himself in a no-budget 1959 picture called *Cuban Rebel Girls*—co-starring his real-life teenage girlfriend, no less. Not to mention Flynn's physical condition in the movie is more than disquieting— at barely 50 years old, he was lined, faintly bloated, and visibly drunk.

Screen Idol

Errol Flynn played swashbuckling heroes many times, but nowhere as effectively as in real life. Tall, athletic, and dashingly handsome, he exuded an easy, irreverent charm that won him fans and friends. An accomplished yachts- man, Flynn also was a novelist, memoirist, inveterate wom- anizer, and Olympian drinker. He was married three times, and after he beat a statutory rape charge in 1943, people began using the expression, "in like Flynn," to signify a person who beat the system, someone too cool for words. Politically, Flynn leaned to the left—no surprise for a man who reveled in excess and answered to no one. While traveling in Cuba in 1958, Flynn became enchanted with Fidel Castro—or perhaps with the *idea* of Castro—and the final push to oust U.S.-supported dictator Fulgencio Batista.

The Actor, the Girl, and the Guerrilla

Accompanying Flynn in Cuba was 16-year-old Beverly Aadland, a baby-faced blonde whom he had chatted up when he met her a year or two prior at the Hollywood Professional School. With Aadland and a small film crew in tow, Flynn ventured into the Sierra Maestra mountains, where he arranged a face-to-face meeting with Castro and filmed the leader and his rebels.

One result of this was a not-bad 50-minute documentary called *Cuban Story*. Since documentaries didn't exactly draw big crowds in 1958, Flynn reasoned that he could cover his travel and production expenses if he spliced some of the real-life footage into a new, fictional story: *Cuban Rebel Girls*.

The Creative Muse

A small cast of unknowns was assembled. Flynn selected Barry Mahon to direct and, nominally, produce the picture. In earlier years, Flynn had worked with some of the best directors in the world, but Mahon's only prior credit was a wretched sci-fi thriller called *Rocket Attack USA*. (Mahon's resume would later include such triumphs as *Pagan Island*, *Nudes Inc.*, and *Prostitutes' Protective Society*.)

Flynn plays himself in *Cuban Rebel Girls*, but not simply as a movie star with a vague political agenda—no, he's a globetrotting adventurer hired by a news service to cover the revolution. As he makes his way into the mountains in the opening of this 68-minute "epic," he encounters Castro, and he chronicles the guerrillas' daily activities via a blend of fact and fabrication. The rebel girls—including the very-blonde Aadland—are as convincing as one might imagine.

Fade to Black

In the film's woeful highlight, Flynn takes a (fake) bullet in the leg and is bandaged by Aadland. Our hero is very obviously drunk in these scenes, unsteady on his feet, and unable to focus on Aadland or anything else. But star power seldom dies out completely; although Flynn appeared older than his years, he still was a good-looking man who managed to summon an ounce of the old sparkle.

Flynn did not live to see the brief theatrical run of *Cuban Rebel Girls*; he died of heart failure in Vancouver on October 14, 1959. An autopsy revealed that more than just Flynn's heart was worn out: Most of the rest of his body—particularly his poor, beleaguered liver—was shot. The doctor remarked that, internally, Flynn's 50-year-old body was that of an elderly man.

Nutty Nietzsche

Plenty of people thought Friedrich Wilhelm Nietzsche was crazy before he actually went mad. Nietzsche's work formed the basis of existentialism, a controversial philosophical movement at a time when religious focus was petering out in intellectual circles. His writing has influenced scores of writers, artists, teachers, and leaders ever since.

The basic idea of Nietzsche's philosophy is quite simple: Human beings are responsible for the creation and meaning of their own lives. When Nietzsche proclaimed his infamous tenet "God is dead," what he meant was that people have the right to believe or not believe in the concept of God because they are responsible for the daily make-up of their own lives and minds. Although Nietzsche's life may have ended in the depths of mental depravity, this fact does not weaken the philosophies he unleashed upon the world in the areas of culture, science, morality, and religion.

A Life of Ups and Downs

Nietzsche was born October 15, 1844, in the Prussian province of Saxony. He was the oldest of three children. Tragically, his father and younger brother died before Nietzsche was seven. For a time it appeared the young boy was destined for a theological career, much to the approval of his mother. At the university in Bonn, he studied theology and philology (the study of how language changes over time), but after one semester Nietzsche rejected his faith and abandoned his theological studies. Needless to say, mama was not pleased. Nietzsche continued his studies in philology and became one of the youngest professors ever to teach the discipline at the University of Basel.

For most of his adult life, Nietzsche was quite sickly. Nevertheless, he served with Prussia as a medical orderly during the Franco-Prussian War of 1870. During this time, he contracted dysentery, diphtheria, and syphilis, the latter of which may have been a cause of his eventual mental illness. Because of these various health woes, Nietzsche had to take a number of sabbaticals, which marked the end of his career as a philologist. Some suggest that these sabbaticals also led to his emergence as a philosopher. There's nothing like being alone in a miserable physical state to make one consider the human condition.

A Genius on His Own Terms

In his immodest, candid, and at times humorous autobiography, *Ecce Homo*, Nietzsche relates in no uncertain terms that he saw in himself how the rest of humanity should be. It's quite possible that Nietzsche really did see himself as *Übermensch*, or superman, a philosophical idea he created in *Thus Spoke Zarathustra*.

Starting to Move Downhill

The first symptoms of serious mental illness surfaced in 1889 on a street in Turin, Italy, when Nietzsche experienced a delirium attack. The experience resulted in Nietzsche's creating a public disturbance that took two police officers to quell. After receiving a brief, puzzling, almost incoherent letter from the philosopher, Franz Overbeck, Nietzsche's closest friend, traveled to Turin and brought him home to Basel, Switzerland, placing him in the care of a psychiatric clinic. Although Nietzsche was displaying many of the signs of mental illness caused by syphilis, he also exhibited some signs that were not. The true cause of his madness is still a matter of conjecture: Did the great thinker's brain blow a fuse from an overload of mental stress, or did his little military stint, turn of patriotism, and possible indiscretion have dire consequences?

Whatever the reason, the man who gave the world pause to think was, at the end, himself completely uncommunicative. Friedrich Wilhelm Nietzsche died of pneumonia on August 25, 1900, while in the care of his sister, proving yet another of his philosophical theories: We are indeed *Human, All Too Human.*

There's More to Know about Tycho

A golden nose, a dwarf, a pet elk, drunken revelry, and, sure, a little bit of astronomy too. Read about the wild life of this groundbreaking astronomer.

Look to the Stars

Tycho Brahe was a Dutch nobleman who is best remembered for blazing a trail in astronomy in an era before the invention of the telescope. Through tireless observation and study, Brahe became one of the first astronomers to fully understand the exact motions of the planets, thereby laying the groundwork for future generations of stargazers.

In 1560, Brahe, then a 13-year-old law student, witnessed a partial eclipse of the sun. He reportedly was so moved by the event that he bought a set of astronomical tools and a copy of Ptolemy's legendary astronomical treatise, *Almagest*, and began a life-long career studying the stars. Where Brahe would differ from his forbearers in this field of study was that he believed that new discoveries in the field of astronomy could be made, not by guesswork and conjecture, but rather by rigorous and repetitious studies. His work would include many publications and even the discovery of a supernova now known as SN 1572.

Hven, Sweet Hven

As his career as an astronomer blossomed, Brahe became one of the most widely renowned astronomers in all of Europe. In fact, he was so acclaimed that when King Frederick II of Denmark heard of Brahe's intention to move to the Swiss city of Basle, the King offered him his own island, Hven, located in the Danish Sound.

Once there, Brahe built his own observatory known as Uraniborg and ruled the island as if it were his own personal kingdom. This meant that his tenants were often forced to supply their ruler (in this case Brahe) with goods and services or be locked up in the island's prison. At one point Brahe imprisoned an entire family—contrary to Danish law.

Did We Mention That
He Was Completely Nutty?

While he is famous for his work in astronomy, Brahe is more infamous for his colorful lifestyle. At age 20, he lost part of his nose in an alcohol-fueled duel (reportedly using rapiers while in the dark) that ensued after a Christmas party. Portraits of Brahe show him wearing a replacement nose possibly made of gold and silver and held in place by an adhesive. Upon the exhumation of his body in 1901, green rings discovered around the nasal cavity of Brahe's skull have also led some scholars to speculate that the nose may actually have been made of copper.

While there was a considerable amount of groundbreaking astronomical research done on Hven, Brahe also spent his time hosting legendarily drunken parties. Such parties often featured a colorful cast of characters including a Little

Person named Jepp who lived under Brahe's dining table and functioned as something of a court jester; it is speculated that Brahe believed that Jepp was clairvoyant. Brahe also kept a tame pet elk, which stumbled to its death after falling down a flight of stairs—the animal had gotten drunk on beer at the home of a nobleman.

Brahe also garnered additional notoriety for marrying a woman from the lower classes. Such a union was considered shameful for a nobleman such as Brahe, and he was ostracized because of the marriage. Thusly all of his eight children were considered illegitimate.

However, the most lurid story of all is the legend that Brahe died from a complication to his bladder caused by not urinating (out of politeness) at a friend's dinner party where prodigious amounts of wine were consumed. The tale lives on, but it should be pointed out that recent research suggests this version of Brahe's demise could be apocryphal: He may have died of mercury poisoning from his own fake nose.

Mean Mommie Joan?

On March 23, 1905, Lucille Fay LeSueur was born in San Antonio, Texas. In her late teens, she joined a traveling theatrical company, and by age 20, she was performing in a chorus line on Broadway.

In 1925, Lucille was contracted by MGM to appear as an extra in six films, receiving her first credit on *Pretty Ladies* (1925). MGM then picked up her option, though studio execs, including Louis B. Mayer, insisted on a name change. In one of the most famous publicity stunts in Hollywood history, MGM held a contest for fans to select a suitable name for her. The starlet made her debut as Joan Crawford in *Old Clothes* (1925).

Crawford did everything the studio asked of her, and more—from appearing in unworthy films to making herself available for all photo opportunities. All of this led MGM screenwriter Frederica Sagor Maas to utter the now-famous words: "No one decided to make Joan Crawford a star. Joan Crawford became a star because Joan Crawford decided to become a star."

Douglas Fairbanks Jr. and the Clark Gable Affair

After a short courtship, Crawford married Douglas Fairbanks Jr. on June 3, 1929. Trouble started brewing when Crawford began filming *Laughing Sinners* (1931), and then *Possessed* (1931), with Clark Gable. Rumors began to circulate that Crawford and Gable were having an affair, and the couple was not discreet with their behavior. Studio execs demanded that the pair curtail the affair, which they did, more or less. But the chemistry between the two was palpable, so the studio cast them in eight films together.

In May 1933, Crawford filed for divorce from Fairbanks, and less than two years later, she married actor Franchot Tone, with whom she appeared in seven films. But the studio made much of Crawford's level of stardom compared to Tone's, which created a lot of tension in the marriage, and the couple filed for divorce in 1939. That same year, Crawford appeared as the villainess in the film *The Women*. She campaigned for the role, and studio execs finally gave it to her, though they disliked the fact that she was playing a hard-edged, unrepentant home wrecker.

Box-Office Poison

In 1932, when the *Motion Picture Herald* released its poll of the top ten moneymaking movie stars, Joan Crawford topped the list. In fact, she held down the top slot in the poll for the next four years. But by 1937, Crawford had not only fallen from the top spot, she didn't even make the top ten. Perhaps that's why the following year, the *Independent Film Journal* referred to her as "box-office poison," though she was in good company because Katharine Hepburn, Greta Garbo, and Marlene Dietrich were also labeled as such by trade magazines in the late 1930s.

Adopting Children

In 1940, although unmarried, Crawford adopted a daughter, Christina. Then, after Crawford married her third husband, Phillip Terry, in July 1942, they adopted another child, Christopher. But when his birth mother found out who had adopted her child, she petitioned the court and was awarded custody. Crawford was outraged and immediately took steps to adopt another boy, whom she named Phillip Terry Jr. When Terry and Crawford divorced in 1946, the eccentric actress received full custody of the two children and legally changed Phillip Jr.'s name to Christopher Crawford. The following year, Crawford adopted two more girls whom she named Cindy and Cathy.

Crawford continued to accept whatever movie roles were offered to her, but they were coming less frequently. In 1943, when her contract with MGM was terminated by mutual consent, Crawford moved to Warner Bros., who gave her more control over her material and directors. Despite the fact that she won a Best Actress Oscar for her role in *Mildred Pierce* (1945) and appeared in a handful of solid dramas, Crawford left Warner Bros. in 1952.

Al Steele and the Pepsi-Cola Company

In May 1955, Crawford married her fourth and final husband, Alfred Steele, the president of Pepsi-Cola. Soon after, Crawford made herself an unofficial spokesperson for Pepsi and began traveling extensively to promote the beverage. When Steele died unexpectedly of a heart attack in 1959, Crawford took his spot on the Board of Directors, even though she had no background in running a business.

In 1961, Crawford was offered a starring role in *What Ever Happened to Baby Jane?* (1962). She played Blanche Hudson, a former A-list actress who had become confined to a wheelchair; Bette Davis portrayed Blanche's sadistic sister. The two actresses were reputedly engaged in a bizarre feud that may have stemmed from the 1930s, when both were interested in Franchot Tone. Legend has it that Crawford complained that Davis intentionally kicked her during a scene. Seeking revenge, Crawford allegedly strapped weights to her body for the scene in which Davis was required to lift her.

Feigning Illness?

When director Robert Aldrich cast Crawford and Davis in *Hush... Hush, Sweet Charlotte* (1964), everyone warned him that he was asking for trouble—and he got it. According to some reports, the two stars were constantly bickering and would often go out of their way to anger each other. Davis seemed to take great pride in trying to get Crawford to snap and appeared to have succeeded when Joan claimed to have fallen ill and left the set. Aldrich begged Crawford to come back, and she did, but when she again claimed she was ill, Aldrich demanded that she be examined by a company physician. Crawford refused and several days later checked into a hospital with an "undisclosed illness." Believing Crawford was faking, Aldrich promptly fired her, scrapped all of the existing footage she appeared in, and replaced her with Olivia de Havilland. Crawford reportedly cried for 39 hours straight after hearing of her replacement.

Turning to Television

With movie scripts no longer coming her way, Crawford turned to the world of television. In 1968, Crawford's daughter Christina, who was also an actress, took medical leave from *The Secret Storm*, the soap opera on which she was a regular. Somehow, Joan convinced producers that she should fill in until Christina returned, despite their 30-year age difference. But during taping, Crawford repeatedly muffed her lines, which caused her to get so angry that she lost it altogether and was reportedly sent home and told not to return.

Joan had several other appearances on TV shows and starred in one final movie, *Trog* (1970), but she was never able to recapture the level of stardom that she once had. Still, by 1972, with her final acting appearance on the TV series *The Sixth Sense*, Crawford's career had spanned an amazing 45 years.

Seclusion and Death

In 1973, when Crawford was told that her services were no longer needed at Pepsi-Cola, she began to withdraw from society. When she saw some unflattering photos of herself at her last known public appearance on September 23, 1974, she is said to have remarked, "If that's how I look, then they won't see me anymore." And with that,

Joan Crawford was rarely seen again until her death on May 10, 1977.

When Crawford's will was read, her two youngest children, Cathy and Cindy, each received roughly $78,000. As for Christina and Christopher, Crawford's will simply stated that "for reasons which are well known to them," they were to receive nothing.

Mommie Dearest

Roughly 18 months after Crawford's death, Christina published *Mommie Dearest*, a book that candidly discussed Joan's (alleged) erratic behavior. (The book was later made into a movie of the same name, starring Faye Dunaway as Crawford.) Christina described how her mother choked her, drank excessively, obsessed over her appearance, and had a revolving door of lovers. But far and away, the most infamous scene in the book (and movie) was the one in which Joan found wire hangers in Christina's closet, which sent Joan into a rage, during which she screamed "No wire hangers! No more wire hangers ever!"

Christina maintains that everything was described in the book exactly as it happened. Crawford's other children and her friends claim that they never saw any of the strange behavior related in the book. True or not, the book has overshadowed Crawford's decades-long career and her glamorous image.